ETHICAL ISSUES IN ECONOMICS

List of Tables

List of Figures

Preface

It was almost twenty years ago, in 1977, when I began my economics undergraduate studies. I was a young left-wing activist, with strong ideological views and values, firmly believing in the possibility of a better world. Indeed, my final choice of economics, instead of my preferred subjects of mathematics and philosophy, had much to do with gaining knowledge and command over what I had learned, from my philosophical studies and Marx in particular, represented society's 'structure' – so that I could then be able to have a 'real' impact on society. Injustices, inequalities and poverty at a national and international level, discrimination, exploitation, greed and corruption . . ., these seemed to me all very real issues that needed to be crucially and urgently tackled, and economics was clearly *the* subject to learn and master in order to do so.

Yet, as an economics undergraduate at the Univerity of Turin, I spent much time writing very outraged comments in the margins of my textbooks, as well as often pestering my own lecturers, even during their (jam-packed) lectures, no doubt disrupting and upsetting them. But I could not accept what I was being generally taught – economic assumptions, models, theories, and all that went with it, from conclusions to policy implications. All seemed to me not so much unrealistic and abstract, as overtly biased in a 'right-wing' direction, offering a picture of economic agents and economic affairs which were in general extremely crude, one-sided and 'immoral'. And this is the background to this book.

My political and moral standing – my belief in the fundamental values of social justice, equality, solidarity, love, altruism, cooperation and duty, own responsibility and rights, honesty, commitment, dignity and respect for others – were, undoubtedly and first of all, highly influenced by my own parents' liberal values and their daily life example of love, generosity, trust and integrity. But they were also clearly formed within my own society's deep Catholic values of love, solidarity and justice, as well as by the strong socialist ideals prevalent in the late 1960s and 1970s of a better, just and equal society, for which we as young people were all fighting. Finally, my humanistic, classic and philosophical studies during my *liceo classico* years provided me with both a fundamental sense of history, a wider perspective on individuals, cultures and societies, and the ability logically and critically to assess and judge other individuals' values, beliefs, opinions, theories, and choices and behaviour.

Family and friends, society, personal experience and learning: these are indeed the underlying elements in any person's formation and 'nature'.

Hence, I would like to express here my gratitude, first of all, to my parents for their love and support throughout my life. The highly animated, often even tumultuous political, philosophical, moral and general discussions with them, and particularly with my father, Giancarlo Lunati, have been a constant major stimulus for developing, testing and deepening my own views.

I would also like to thank my good and old friend Brian Hillier for kindly 'putting up' with me since the days of my D.Phil. supervision at the University of York; and more seriously and more to the point, for originally encouraging me to write this book, although (I must stress) he bears no responsibility whatsoever for its content – indeed, as a mainstream economist himself, he rather disagrees with much of what I say.

My economics colleagues at Bolton Business School, and especially Barry Simmons, also merit my sincere thanks for helping me out with some teaching while I was otherwise engaged with the book.

Last but not least, I would like to thank genuinely my husband, Andy Reed, for his emotional and practical support while I was writing the book, as well as for generously coping with my (related) stress and 'occasional' bad temper. Life might have been very 'solitary and poor' (although not necessarily 'nasty, brutish and short') without him at my side.

Two methodological issues concerning the book should be discussed here. The first regards a matter that may be called one of 'political correctness'. Up to the very last draft, all chapters strictly adhered to this rule insofar as references to *an individual* were made. Hence, the 'he/she' or 'him/her' notation was omnipresent. Indeed an additional element – perhaps not so politically correct but rather gender-biased – was present. Namely, whenever the individual being discussed was altruistic and/or cooperative, then that individual was a definite she; whereas when selfish and/or non-cooperative, then the individual was a sure he. In other words, *homo economicus* was a man, while *homo ethicus* a woman. However, in the final version of the book, the 'non-politically correct' stance has been adopted, dropping all he/she and him/her references (as well as the 'biased' notation), and this for three basic reasons. Firstly, to 'save words', as I was somewhat under pressure not to exceed my given (though rather generous) allowance of 80,000 words. Secondly and more seriously, as a matter of writing 'style', for I have always felt the 'he/she, him/her' wording to be rather burdensome and unattractive. Moreover, as an Italian I was educated by the old classic school that any reference to a generic (sexually unspecified) individual would always be made in the masculine gender as a pure matter of language convention. And I still believe that some old linguistic (stylistic) rules have a lot going for them, when compared to some new fashionable ones. Finally, from a 'truly' political (and feminist) perspective, I do not believe for a moment that women's position in the world is going to be improved by replacing some old male-oriented words with new double-gender neutral ones. To effect such an improvement, I feel that what is needed, above all, is a genuinely more altruistic, cooperative and equitable world.

The second issue concerns footnotes, references and quotes. Most chapters have, to a greater or lesser extent, numerous footnotes attached, as well as extensive references and citations. At times, footnotes simply refer to literature references; but at others they contain material of a substantive and/or clarifying nature, which might nevertheless be passed over by a more hasty reader, without risk of misapprehending the main argument. As to the references themselves, they are by no means comprehensive of all relevant existing literature. Yet an effort was made to include, or possibly even just mention, most of those that might be regarded as fundamental in a specific area, as well as some that might be thought of as marginal and yet somehow provide some significant contribution to the debate. Finally, the use of frequent quotations from several authors is due to a number of reasons. Besides the obvious one of avoiding any risk of plagiarism, a more fundamental reason is to provide the reader with direct literature-based support, or conversely counter-views, to the arguments being made. Also, in a few chapters, it is the specific works of some authors which is the analytical focus, and hence direct quotation from them seems the rather natural way to proceed.

Acknowledgements

I wish to thank Dr Victor Mok, editor of the *Journal of Economic Methodology* (formerly *Methodus*) for permission to reprint my article 'On Altruism and Cooperation', originally published in *Methodus*, 4 (2) December, pp. 69–75, 1992. It appears here, under a different title and slightly amended, as Chapter 4.

I would also like to thank Mrs Penny Dole, copy-editor for Macmillan, for her valuable editorial assistance.

Introduction

GENERAL OVERVIEW

This book focuses on a number of ethical issues and ethical values, as well as moral norms and moral dispositions relevant to economic theory, and in particular to economic agents' beliefs, behaviour and activity. And, as the morality of individuals influences their economic conduct and choices, their morality is also clearly relevant to socio-economic policies and outcomes.

The book is not meant as a treatise on 'ethics and economics'. Hence, it is not intended to cover all ethical aspects relevant to economic analysis, or economic aspects with ethical implications; nor is it aimed at providing an overview of the wide spectre of economic–ethical–theoretical interdependencies. More modestly, the book aims to offer a critical perspective on a selected number of economically relevant (and useful) ethical human qualities and values – notably altruism, cooperation and equity.

Broadly speaking, the book has three main objectives. First, it seeks to analyse and question the standard position of mainstream neoclassical economics on fundamental issues such as 'selfishness vs altruism', 'non-cooperation vs cooperation' and 'efficiency vs equity' – issues which all have a clear 'moral' content. A second and related objective is to analyse the implications of this 'orthodox' position in terms of: economic theory's explanations and predictions; 'rational' individuals' presumed preferences or objectives and expected choices and behaviour; policy-makers' and politicians' induced policy choices; as well as economics students' potentially 'biased' learning. Third, it seeks to analyse and discuss the 'legitimacy' and implications of alternative ('socio-economic' or 'moral-economic') positions on those issues – positions which, unlike the standard traditional view, address the 'moral dimension' of economic analysis, typically taking explicit account of economic *and* non-economic (social, cultural, political, historical and ethical) factors that affect human nature and hence, in turn, influence the analysis.

The mainstream of modern economic theory is, as is well known, built upon the fundamental premise that individuals, as economic agents, are selfish non-cooperative rational utility- (or profit)maximizers acting in isolation: namely, *homines economici* or, as they are also known, *homines rationales*. The underlying assumptions about individuals' behaviour and choices thus reflect a 'particular' view about human nature, a view which does not generally allow for moral values – such as altruism, cooperation, commitment, duty, fairness, justice, equity – to enter into individuals' intentions or motivations when acting in the economic sphere and taking decisions about their own and other peoples' lives. For, according to standard neoclassical economic theory, all economic behaviour can be understood as the rational pursuit of self-interest.

The 'free-rider' problem, the 'Prisoner's Dilemma' paradox, the economic well-known dictum 'there is no such a thing as a free lunch', and (perhaps above all) Adam Smith's (1776) famous words: 'It is not from the benevolence of the butcher, the brewer, or the baker, that we expect our dinner, but from their regard to their own interest. We address ourselves not to their humanity but to their self-love, and never talk to them of our own necessities but of their advantages.' These are all examples which well exemplify orthodox economists' 'belief' in a particular type of *humanity*: one of individuals who are actually not very nice (if not indeed nasty), and who cannot and should not, after all, be expected to be nice.

Individuals' 'niceness' or 'kindness' – meaning a caring and cooperative behaviour, and one that is also influenced or determined by ethical values or moral norms of fairness, equity, justice, sense of duty, responsibility, commitment, honesty, loyalty, trust, goodwill . . . – is, in fact, not consistent with 'economic rationality', and is hence generally interpreted as a sign of irrationality or of weakness. Indeed, the common saying 'nice guys finish last' seems to capture well this economic conception and economists' deep conviction.

Also, the main (and often regarded as the only proper) criterion of economic valuation, efficiency, is typically presumed to conflict with the other criterion, equity, thus implying that the latter can only be traded-off against costly losses in the former. 'Fair' or 'equitable' outcomes are seen as a matter of subjective normative valuation involving moral judgements, and are hence taken to be discretionary and non-objective – unlike 'efficient' outcomes that are normally presumed to be objective, positive, technical, scientific, value-free and morally neutral.

Mainstream neoclassical economists, unlike other social scientists, hold the belief that the behaviour of individuals, as *Rational Economic Men*, can be explained and indeed predicted by assuming that individuals have set and stable (egoistic and well-defined) preferences and make rational choices consistent with those preferences. Clearly, an *ex-post* explanation of individuals' choices or behaviour can always be found or given. But whether such an explanation helps in understanding why individuals did actually choose what they did or behaved as they did, that is, their intentions or motivations, is a different matter. For the *ex-post* explanation can be an *ad hoc* or a functional or instrumental one, simply confirming what the economist believes in or 'requires' for the choice made by the individual to conform with economic 'instrumental rationality' or expected utility theory. Moreover, this explanatory method seems to also imply a *de facto* denial of individuals' 'free will'. For if the individual, *given* his (presumed) utility function and preferences and the constraints he faces, is shown to have *necessarily* made the best/correct decisions by choosing what he actually did, then it is obviously implied that the individual could not have chosen any other option. Alternatively, the implication is that, if the individual in that particular situation had chosen a different option, then he would not have made the optimal/correct choice – for his behaviour would not have been in line with rational self-interested utility-maximizing behaviour, and this would be due to possible ignorance, lack of information, misinformation or else, and more likely, 'irrationality'. But as Sen (1987) remarks: 'To see any departure from self-interest maximization as evidence of irrationality must imply a rejection of the role of ethics in actual decision taking' (p. 15).

Indeed, whenever an individual's behaviour is not consistent with his presumed preferences, and hence, as Camerer and Thaler (1995) put it, 'it is difficult to "rationalize" or if implausible assumptions are necessary to explain it within the paradigm' (p. 209), then such behaviour or empirical result qualifies as an 'anomaly'. However, the problem with the standard assumptions of 'rational choice'/expected utility theory is, in Aaron's (1994) words, that: 'Much (perhaps most) human behaviour violates these standards.' And after adding a long list of these alleged 'irrationalities', Aaron goes on to remark that, in fact: 'These so-called "paradoxes" or "anomalies" are pervasive' (p. 9). Thus, as Frank (1996) argues: 'In the end, traditional economists must weigh the satisfaction they take in clinging to narrow versions of the rational choice model against the inability of that model to account for important categories of human behaviour' (p. 118).[1]

What if individuals' behaviour and choices that appear to mainstream economists as 'anomalies' are indeed *normal* behaviour and choices?

What if, in other words, anomalous behaviours are only so within and because of the standard economic framework? And what if, in order to explain or predict human behaviour, including economic behaviour, we were to abandon the utilitarian emphasis on '(self-)interest' or 'utility', and adopt instead the Kantian emphasis on 'duty', or in general an emphasis on 'morality'? Clearly, several important implications would follow.[2]

It is ironic that mainstream neoclassical economists struggle so much to be and to be seen as objective positivist 'scientists'. For the theory they so passionately espouse is essentially built and then developed on an 'act of faith' and several 'dogmas'. These being, namely, the faith in the utilitarian, rationalistic, individualistic, hedonistic and self-centred neoclassical doctrine-credo of *laissez-faire*, and, in turn, the dogmas about all its related core assumptions or axioms concerning individuals' preferences and behaviour. Thus, standard orthodox economists often resemble much more religious dogmatic or even fanatical believers than scientific scholars. And economic 'fundamentalism' often seems to replace lucid economic reasoning.

Moreover, since neoclassical economists believe in the allegedly objective, positive, 'scientific' nature of economic theory (without seemingly recognizing its implicit right-wing ideological and political bias), their attitude and approach towards other disciplines is, as a result, crucially affected. Thus, they are, for example, generally ready to accept, and even incorporate into their theory, some not strictly economic but purportedly *scientific* psychological factors or theories – as, for example, 'risk aversion' or 'regret' theory – which deal with individuals' supposedly 'innate' or intrinsic or even genetical characteristics or nature. Similarly, the strong and increasing appeal amongst economists of (socio)biological/evolutionary theories is not surprising, as these theories also appear to provide a *scientific* foundation to economic theorizing. But economists do not generally accept, and are not even willing to contemplate, the possibility of ethical conduct by economic agents or the economic relevance of moral issues – for this would shift the analysis of individual behaviour and (macro)economic issues onto philosophical and possibly political, and hence 'unscientific' grounds.[3]

The separation between economics and ethics, as well as between economics and politics, and indeed their mutual independence, are tenets strongly held by economists, for their denial would seriously compromise the 'scientific' nature of economics, throwing inadmissible doubts on the validity of core economic theories and well-established economic results. What can be and normally is accepted by economists is the influence of ethics and politics on specific but quite distinct economic areas, such as welfare economics and, notably, political economy. But these areas, and the latter in particular, are in fact typically regarded by modern mainstream economists as not proper economic subject areas – although this view was clearly not shared by the classical and early neoclassical economists, from Adam Smith to David Ricardo to Thomas Malthus to John Stuart Mill to Karl Marx, who were all political economists, as well as (moral) philosophers and political theorists. Similarly, according to Keynes (1973): 'Economics is essentially a moral science and not a natural science. That is to say, it employs introspection and judgments of value' (p. 297), and 'it deals with motives, expectations, psychological uncertainties' (p. 300). And as Sen (1987) argues, economics 'can be made more productive by paying greater and more explicit attention to the ethical considerations that shape human behaviour and judgement' (p. 9).

By contrast, non-orthodox economists have long recognized that the positive-normative distinction of economic analysis is mostly fictitious, for positive and normative economic issues are normally intermingled. Also, that economics is not a 'scientific' discipline, as are physics, chemistry or biology (whereas orthodox economists would typically mantain that economics is a 'science', not because of its subject matter, but because of its methodology).[4] And that economic analysis, whether theoretical or empirical, is generally inescapably affected by the moral and political views, prejudices or judgements of the researchers, of their schools and even of their own societies, by way of either influencing their selection of topics or problems to study, or their approach to and evaluation of them. As Frank (1996) asks in this regard: 'Do scientists evaluate theories and evidence independently and disinterestedly, as they would like to believe, or do social influences intrude even in this hallowed domain?' (p. 121). His answer is that: 'The power of social forces to enshrine manifestly false beliefs in science is not to be underestimated. The economics profession, for all its pretensions of being an objective science, is hardly immune' (p. 122).[5]

More generally, non-orthodox economists do openly acknowledge the interdependence between economics, ethics and politics, rather than ignoring or even denying it. As a result, their areas of research and/or their research methodology are frequently different from those of mainstream orthodox economics. Although, as Frank (1996) notes: 'As long as the received scientific wisdom favors a given theory, someone who speaks out against it risks being thought incompetent or ill-informed' (p. 122).

All this, in turn, results in several 'unfortunate' outcomes. Firstly, a gap emerges between the two groups, orthodox and non-orthodox economists, with little (if any) communication being exchanged between them. Secondly, since mainstream neoclassical economists form the large majority, non-orthodox economists risk or tend to be marginalized or ignored, or even discriminated against in various direct or indirect ways – through their feeble publication chances in 'core' mainstream journals, and their consequently impaired academic work and career prospects. The well-known 'publish or perish' academic maxim does thus effectively put an end to most non-orthodox research ambitions or attempts, especially by young researchers, except for a few strong-minded, (usually left-wing) politically-oriented and/or highly-ethical, if naive, economic scholars. Finally, and possibly most importantly, the only voice normally heard in the public arena and having a significant impact on economic policies and outcomes is that of the mainstream neoclassical economists, with all its natural consequences on the economy and society as a whole – good or bad, beneficial or damaging, depending obviously on individuals' own socio-economic circumstances and/or political and ethical perspective. For, clearly, different explanations of the causes and effects of, say, inflation or unemployment will naturally result in different policy measures/recommendations – where not only may the actual economic policy effects be more or less close to the predicted ones, but also the policy intended distributional impact may well vary substantially, favouring certain individuals or groups rather than others.

OVERVIEW OF CHAPTERS

The first three chapters focus on several aspects closely related to the issue of altruism. Chapter 1 discusses the link between altruism, morality and rationality sustaining the view of morality as 'altruism *cum* rationality', as well as the link between morality, the 'Invisible Hand' theory and individual freedom. Chapter 2 analyses the two standard economic approaches to altruism – of 'putting it into the individual utility function', or 'equating it with cooperative behaviour'; and then considers alternative socio-economic or moral-economic approaches, favouring the latter, albeit this leaves open the question of how to model formally altruism in economic analysis. Chapter 3 looks at the specific treatment of altruism in a sample of recent economic works, and at the consequent (typically negative and/or highly questionable) implications of such a treatment both for an altruist himself and for economic outcomes in general. A Supplement to Chapter 3 considers some logical (if paradoxical) developments of the sociobiological theory of altruism.

Chapter 4 addresses the issue of ethical and political non-neutrality of mainstream neoclassical economics, focusing on its key assumptions about human nature, as encapsulated in the theory of *homo economicus*. It then considers the legitimacy of a 'reverse' postulate – of an altruistic, cooperative and socially integrated individual, who might be termed *homo ethical*; and looks at several implications for economic analysis and policy of such an alternative postulate.

The next two chapters discuss the need for a moral assessment of economics in all its numerous facets. Chapter 5 starts with a discussion of the interdependence between ethics, politics and economics, arguing for the need to re-establish the supremacy of ethics over the others. It then moves to a moral valuation of economic research, teaching and forecasting, as well as looking at some 'semantic' issues in economics. The Supplement to Chapter 5 is directly concerned with the 'nature' of economists, and the negative or corrupting effects that studying economics seems to have on students. Chapter 6 turns to a moral assessment of game theory, and then considers the possible meaning of 'mixed' results in economic laboratory experiments, concluding with a discussion of 'teleological' versus 'deontological' ethics.

Chapter 7 analyses the two alternative approaches to the problem of how to explain or justify cooperation in situations of conflict of interests amongst individuals – such as the 'Prisoner's Dilemma' or other Social Dilemmas. The first – the standard economic and game-theoretic approach that presupposes 'rational, self-interested' motivations – is briefly discussed, and four types of 'competitive' individuals are considered. The main focus is, though, on the second approach – which is to view cooperation as driven by 'moral' motivations. Different moral principles or rules prescribing cooperation as the norm are thus analysed, with secular or religious morality seen as the clear source of social cooperative behaviour. Six types of 'cooperative' – 'ethical' or 'biblical' – individuals emerge from the analysis and their relative cooperative strength is also assessed.

Chapter 8 focuses on the relationship between equity and efficiency, and in turn between equity and economic growth. The three theoretical cases of a positive or negative relationship or independence are considered, and the rationale behind each hypothesis is analysed both from an economic and political/ethical perspective. The emphasis of standard neoclassical economics on a 'trade-off' between efficiency and equity is contrasted with theoretical arguments and evidence in favour of a positive link – suggesting that a more equitable distribution of income should be advocated not only on political or moral grounds, but also on strong economic grounds.

The final chapter offers a brief review of the main features and values of *neoclassical* economic men, firms and markets, as compared to those (different and indeed quite opposite) of *ethical* men, firms and markets. Believing in the possible realization of an *ethical society* may well be seen as utopian, but ideals are nonetheless fundamental to human beings and certainly worth striving for. Utopia may yet one day come true.

1 Altruism, Rationality and Morality

INTRODUCTION

When looking at the growing interest amongst economists in altruism and its economic implications, one question may quite naturally be raised. Why is so much of economic literature, in more recent years at least, on the one hand, increasingly incorporating altruism into formal analysis and models, while seemingly trying, on the other hand, to 'discredit' altruism? This is typically done by, for example, showing that altruism can result in inefficient resource allocations and inefficient outcomes – as in the 'Samaritan's dilemma' context, with the possible (or likely) exploitation of, or 'free-riding' on, the altruism of others by selfish individuals; and/or by modelling altruism in a 'non-altruistic' manner.[1]

A possible answer is that it may be a deliberate or unconscious attempt by economists to provide an explanation or justification for individuals' allegedly widespread selfishness and self-interested behaviour. Also, it may be an attempt to, indirectly at least, 'elevate' self-interest as a *de facto* superior motive for action, compared to altruism; that is to say, re-establish the 'value' of selfishness, while also legitimizing it: if altruism may result in 'unfortunate' economic outcomes, then surely egoism is not so bad, after all. And, what is possibly more important, the 'value' of selfishness may re-emerge not only in economic terms, but also in moral/ethical terms, for altruism is typically equated with moral behaviour. Indeed, Collard's (1978, pp. 6–7) defence of self-interest is on 'normative or welfare economics' grounds – as it leads to socially good outcomes; on 'positive economics' grounds – as it leads to good empirical predictions; *and* on 'moral' grounds – as its motives are not ignoble. Clearly, if the economic pursuit of non-selfish or altruistic aims results in 'bad' outcomes, then, it may well be argued, one ought to pursue *only* one's own interest – as a positive moral obligation, and not just as a moral permission. Self-interest thus becomes a moral principle, instead of simply being, as usually presumed or maintained, a morally neutral concept.[2]

A problem with this attempt is that, far from really providing an understanding of why individuals are or may be selfish, the potential if unintended implication is to nurture and enhance individuals' selfishness by providing rational motivations for it. Moreover, there are here two additional conceptual problems. The first is a misguided and confusing equation of altruism with morality.[3] For, it will be argued here, it is only *altruism cum rationality* that can give rise to morality – as also argued by, for example, Alberoni and Veca (1988), and somewhat similarly by Collard (1992).[4] The second conceptual problem is an implicit and highly questionable identification of morality with 'instrumental (functionalist) rationality' – utilitarian morality. (See Section 1.2 below, for a discussion of the different meaning of altruism and rationality, as typically understood by economists and as, conversely, intended here.)

Moreover and partly related to the previous point, this 'double-dealing' with altruism seems to be a result of the mainstream neoclassical economists' separation between economics and ethics, which involves the ethics-less view of economics, and in general the view that economics is a scientific, objective, value-free, positive discipline, whose main (if not only) proper concern and criterion of valuation is economic efficiency – in terms of allocation of (scarce) resources. Thus, according to this standard economic position, we may, as economists, allow for the existence of altruistic individuals. But, in the strictly economic sphere, the role of altruism cannot (and should not) be exaggerated. For the fundamental motive underlying individuals' economic activity is rational self-interest, as properly exemplified by the nature and behaviour of *homo economicus*. Altruism may at best be a secondary economic motive, although altruism no doubt underlies moral judgements.[5] But equity or distributional considerations, and more generally moral considerations, are better left to policy makers and moral philosophers.

In the next three sections, various aspects of the relationship between altruism, rationality and morality are discussed, while Section 1.4 focuses on moral behaviour in relation to the 'invisible hand' operation and, in turn, individual freedom.

1.1 MORALITY AS 'ALTRUISM *CUM* RATIONALITY'

According to Jerome Kagan (1984), 'the problem on which most moral philosophers have stubbed their toes' has been the '(c)onstruction of a persuasive rational basis for behaving morally'; while they should, in his opinion, simply recognize that 'feeling, not logic, sustains the superego'. Thus, in order to explain moral behaviour, Kagan appeals to human feelings – while some might here suggest instincts, impulses, passions, emotions, sentiments or other similar psychological mental states or biological human traits, with the alternative clearly being an appeal to human logic. For, as Frank (1987, p. 602) argues – having also quoted Kagan (1984) – 'Feelings may indeed sustain the superego. But . . . it is logic that ultimately sustains those feelings.' And, in support of logic, it could also be argued that the main distinctive trait or characteristic of individuals, as compared to animals, is indeed their ability and capacity to use their 'reason', and to 'pass rational judgements' and moral judgements in particular – instead of being simply led by innate and possibly irrational forces.

The idea that 'behaving morally' needs a rational basis (explanation or justification) no doubt also rests on the implicit assumption or consideration that 'behaving immorally' may (well) bring a better 'individual outcome' – which, in turn, is supposed to be the 'motivational force' of individual behaviour, according in particular to the instrumental rational-choice theory of selfish conduct. If behaviour is to be judged in terms of its consequences/outcomes – that is, instrumentally – then, clearly, a 'moral behaviour' has also to be evaluated for its results, and has hence to be similarly founded on rational grounds. In other words, this line of reasoning implies the need to rationally motivate a 'moral behaviour'.

Certainly, the 'Kantian principle' – the categorical imperative – for being moral and behaving morally is based upon 'reason', and not upon love (as also underlined by Collard (1978, p. 14)). But morality or moral behaviour do not, in general, necessarily require to be rationally justified. This is not to deny that 'rationality' is a component of morality. Indeed, as Alberoni and Veca (1988) put it, rationality is one of the two roots of morality, alongside altruism – while each one on its own is not necessarily moral. In other words, both altruism *and* rationality are necessary conditions for morality, but neither is a sufficient condition.

Why should I, one might ask, explain or indeed justify, and to whom, my behaving morally? For my moral behaviour, one might indeed answer, I ought to be accountable only to myself. Moreover, the very need to explain or justify (supposedly) moral behaviour may even, in theory, deny or contradict the nature of such behaviour as moral.

Moral behaviour has to be based upon 'reason', as well as upon 'altruism' or love. However, the search or quest for a rational foundation of moral behaviour seems to be intrinsically linked to an utilitarian conception of rationality *and* morality. In other words, the need to find a rational basis for moral behaviour is a clearly utilitarian (and typically Anglo-Saxon) need. But it is also a Kantian need.

According to Kant, it is 'reason', which is common to all human beings, that obliges us to act upon *duty*. And moreover, for Kant, the moral 'universal principle' of duty rests only upon reason, and not upon love. But, as Alberoni and Veca (1988) remark, duty is an *as if* of love.[6] In the absence of sentiment (love), reason can certainly inherit from it the altruistic intention and equally realize it. The moral act is, in this way, de-subjectivized. Rational morality has, hence, substituted duty for love. But, although the 'morality of duty' has great merits, the ultimate outcome of this process of objectivization is the robot. Moreover, while the morality of love is a morality of joy, the morality of duty is a morality of effort. And, if it is true that 'altruism without reason is blind', it is also true that 'reason without altruism is empty' – indeed, moral behaviour purely based upon rationality, without love (as, one might argue, the Anglo-Saxon (stereo)type-behaviour), can be very 'cold', apart from being empty.

Moral behaviour, according to Alberoni and Veca (1988), arises from an 'independent moral stimulus':[7] an impulse independent, that is, from rationality, and that makes one choose altruism instead of egoism, independently moreover of whether such moral behaviour will (or might), in the long run at least, turn to one's own advantage – as utilitarianism would, on the contrary, maintain.

Why should I, one might also ask, behave morally, if by behaving immorally I could, probably if not surely, be better off? An answer here is that I could certainly be better off in material terms – that is, my utility could be higher. Hence, behaving morally would be instrumentally 'irrational'. But if my utility also includes 'moral preferences', then I could, in theory and in practice, be worse off, in terms of my 'total utility'. And, moreover, if mine is not a 'utility-maximizing' behaviour, but for example a behaviour based on a 'deontological' morality, then the resulting level of my utility could be a non-determinant of, or even irrelevant to, my chosen behaviour.

1.2 ALTRUISM AND RATIONALITY

When dealing with altruism, two misplaced identities are commonly made: the first, already mentioned and partially discussed, is a wrong identification of altruism with 'morality'; the second, and in part as a result of the first, is a wrong identification of altruism with 'charitable giving'.

I may well be a strong, genuine altruist (my degree (intensity) and domain (extent) of altruism may, in other words, be very high and wide, respectively), and yet I might never, in general, give money to charity – since such an act may, indeed, be *against* my moral principles. My morality (*altruism cum rationality*) might, however, make me willing and ready to pay more taxes – the belief that 'no one likes paying taxes, whereas people generally feel good about donating money to famine relief or the church roof fund', as Miller claims (1988, p. 163), would certainly be wrong in this case. For my 'moral reasoning' can make me understand that it is only through collective action, and not individualistic philanthropy, that society's 'needs' (in a general sense) can be appropriately met.

Indeed, 'individual charitable giving' can be interpreted or judged as, at best, non-rational morality, and, at worst, as a non-truly altruistic act. Hence, there is here a possible truth in the economists' cynical interpretation of charitable giving, as ultimately, deep down, self-interested (or enlightened self-interest) behaviour. True, genuine concern for other individuals' needs or welfare, properly supported by 'reason' and so underpinning rational morality, should in fact rule out charity. For charity: (i) can be inefficient, and (ii) can be said to be against the recipients' *human dignity*, a highly important and indeed fundamental moral value.[8]

Thus, according to rational morality, the 'unfortunate' or 'unhappy' outcomes of altruism – that altruism may well be a counterproductive social force resulting in 'damaging' outcomes for the 'objects' of one's love, and in inefficient allocative outcomes – are not, as many economists claim, paradoxical or 'surprising'. Rather, these 'bad' outcomes are simply the consequence of the fact that *altruism without rationality* does not generate moral behaviour. For an altruist may or may not be rational, likewise an egoist. And altruism may not be moral, unless it is supported by 'reason'/rationality.

Clearly, 'rationality' here is not that endorsed by economists as 'instrumental rationality theory' – (expected) utility theory. For utility theory is not – or, in Hausman and McPherson's (1993, p. 688) less definite view, 'may not even be' – compatible with moral behaviour. Rather, the rationality concept highlighted here is the individual capacity to evaluate (morally) own personal goals, aims and behaviour in a lucid manner. In other words, 'being rational' here means being able logically to assess or evaluate a situation and/or an action to be taken – and not being driven by pure (non-rational or even irrational) instincts, impulses, passions, feelings or emotions in one's judgement or action; but without making any commitment to an individual (self-interested) utility-maximizing goal or behaviour. Moreover, 'rationality' here does also involve an evaluation by the individual of his own ends, and not simply of the means to achieve those ends – as, conversely, implicit in the economic conception of 'instrumental rationality', of choosing efficiently the means to satisfy individual subjective preferences that, in line with Hume's (1740) theory of motivation, are in themselves not necessarily rational, as not given by reason and not themselves subject to rational appraisal.[9]

Indeed, if a 'rational altruist' is simply taken to mean (in the orthodox economic sense) an altruist who is able to calculate his first-order conditions for utility maximization – where the altruist's utility does also include another person's utility – then the unfortunate outcomes or resource allocation inefficiencies may well result. But altruism should *not* be in the utility function. And rationality should *not* be identified with instrumental utility theory or self-interest. For 'rational altruism' *is* morality and, as Alberoni and Veca (1988) remark, morality is, really, the suppression of the calculus of own utility.

Moreover, it is the very notion of altruism as altruism toward some specific person(s) that makes it, arguably, 'non rational' and 'non moral'. That is, 'narrow' altruism can certainly generate inefficiencies. But true, genuine altruism cannot be narrow, since true altruism can only mean concern and love for others, where the other is anyone in general, and not someone in particular. This view is clearly contrary to that typically held by economists (as well as sociobiologists and some moral philosophers), that altruism is conceivable and indeed natural towards some other individuals, such as family members or members of some larger group. But, in the common economic view and as Collard (1978, p. 12) argues: 'Generalised altruism towards the human race is rare and, indeed, suspect.' Although, as Collard then admits, 'there is also a generalised concern, not towards mankind as an abstraction, but towards particular types of need by socially distant and unknown other individuals', and indeed, '(t)he prime factor here is sympathetic identification' (p. 12).[10]

1.3 MORALITY AND RATIONALITY

When considering the relationship between morality and rationality, two crucial questions can be raised – as raised, for example, by Hausman and McPherson (1993, pp. 679–89). The first is whether it is sometimes irrational to act morally. The second is whether it is sometimes immoral to act rationally. These questions can be answered straightforwardly, once it is accepted that morality is *altruism cum rationality*. (Thus, the answers here somewhat differ from those given by Hausman and McPherson (1993), as they do not embrace exactly the same view of morality.) The answer to the first question – is it sometimes irrational to act morally? – is that *it is not possible or true*: acting morally requires also, by definition, acting rationally. Hence, acting morally could be said to be irrational, only if moral behaviour were 'mistakenly' assumed not to require the component of 'rationality', and/or if 'rationality' were stricly identified with self-interest/instrumental rationality/utility theory. The answer to the second question – is it sometimes immoral to act rationally? – is that *it is possible and may sometimes be true*: rationality *per se* (on its own, without altruism) does not entail morality. This may especially be true if 'rationality' is taken to mean self-interest, but it can also be true when 'rationality' is interpreted in the different way put forward here. For, to reiterate, only if rationality is 'accompanied' by altruism, can individual behaviour be said to be moral.

1.4. MORAL BEHAVIOUR AND THE 'INVISIBLE HAND', AND INDIVIDUAL FREEDOM

Adam Smith's 'invisible hand' theory – which ensures that the individual pursuit of self-interest is in the society's general interest – represents, undoubtedly, a major contribution to economic analysis and an extremely important economic result, in terms of economic efficiency at least.[11] But it is not a moral result, for two fundamental reasons. First, self-interest can certainly be said to be natural, rational and legitimate, but is not moral or morally neutral – as Alberoni and Veca (1988) put it more forcefully, 'egoism is, by definition, immoral'. And second, the 'invisible hand' operation – in which individuals in pursuing their own interests *unintentionally and unknowingly* promote the public interest or social good, *as if* led by an invisible hand – implicitly neglects or ignores individuals' true intentions, with the best possible social outcome resulting, in fact, as an unintended, unconscious and involuntary, albeit desirable if somewhat miraculous, consequence of individual behaviour. Therefore, the 'invisible hand' mechanism can be said to 'remove' individual effective freedom of action, or, perhaps more importantly here, responsibility for own action, and hence entails a denial of moral behaviour.[12]

Indeed, this argument points to an apparent *paradox* in orthodox economic theorizing with respect to individual freedom. On the one hand, neoclassical economists typically value individual freedom highly (as so clearly did Adam Smith), and in particular the individual 'freedom of choice' that the market mechanism is claimed to promote and guarantee.[13] In fact, as Etzioni (1988, p. 10) argues, this is the very reason for the neoclassical assumption that 'free-standing individuals are the decision-making units, the actors', implying the atomization of the economic agents, with each acting independently in isolation – hence conventional economists' commitment to *methodological individualism.* And the main implication of this social and political philosophy of libertarian 'radical individualism' for the role of the community is – in Bentham's (1789) words, also quoted by Etzioni (1988) – that: 'The community is a fictitious body, composed of . . . individual persons.' Moreover, the same deep commitment to the value of liberty is also at the root of the neoclassical assumption that individuals' preferences are given, and individuals know best what is best for them and know their own mind. For, according to neoclassical economists, to assume that preferences are not given, but can be changed or are in part socially shaped, implies that preferences can be manipulated by social or political forces, and this undermines the foundations of liberty.[14] And, as Etzioni (1988, p. 137) goes on to argue, the commitment to liberty is also the deeper reason for the neoclassical assumption 'that individuals "must be" rational, "must be" able to form their own judgments, and that their choices must be perceived as basically morally correct'. For 'neoclassicists believe that any other position would justify a curtailment of individual rights'. Thus, neoclassicists maintain, individual 'rationality' must be assumed, for, 'to assume otherwise, is to assume that people make unwise or morally deficient choices, and to suggest that they can be manipulated', and 'this systematically opens the door to government intervention, if not to totalitarianism'.

On the other hand, however, neoclassical economists believe that free unfettered individuals will normally render optimal decisions, in similarly free unfettered markets – which, if only left to themselves and not interfered with by the government, operate in an optimal Pareto-efficient manner, hence always eventually clearing; and moreover, that these individual decisions will turn out to be optimal not only for the individual decision-makers themselves, but also for the society as a whole, hence leading to a harmonious social order – by virtue of the operation of the always present and providential 'invisible hand'. But all these beliefs together appear to contradict the very idea that individuals are 'free to choose', particularly in the Kantian sense of being *autonomous*, as rational self-legislators – besides denying individuals the possibility of behaving morally.

More specifically, the only things individuals seem to be possibly 'free to choose' in such a context are their own utility functions or preferences. Indeed, according to neoclassical economic theory, the individual has *given* preferences and these are, in fact, taken as a given (as fixed, set and stable) by the economist, and moreover as not subject to rational (moral) appraisal, either by the economist or by the same individual whose preferences they are. And, at the same time, these individual preferences are also typically assumed to be associated with pleasure, happiness or satisfaction resulting from consumption, hence commodity-related: they are basically tastes or wants of some commodity, that is, 'first-order' or 'lower' preferences – in contrast to 'second-order' or 'higher-order' preferences or 'meta-preferences', relating to individual values and beliefs. Therefore, it is very much a 'market choice', or indeed 'consumer choice', the freedom of choice that a free-market *laissez-faire* economy is supposed to intrinsically promote – as opposed to the morally valuable concept of freedom as individual *autonomy* or self-determination.[15]

Moreover, according to standard rational-choice theory, preferences are assumed to be 'revealed through choices'. Thus, once individuals have made up their minds about their own utility function – that is, what types of commodity they desire for providing them with satisfaction – then, given the constraints they face and in particular their budget constraint, their 'rationality' – in the economic instrumental sense of self-interested utility maximization – will clearly and unequivocally indicate to them how to behave, in terms of the optimal rational choices they have to make. In other words, individuals will rationally choose their actions or behaviour on the basis of their *given* preferences. In Simon's (1986, p. 27) words: 'The rational person of neoclassical economics always reaches the decision that is objectively, or substantively, best in terms of the given utility function.' Furthermore, this also implies that if the economist knows an individual's utility function and constraints, then the economist can clearly predict the choices that that individual, as a rational decision-maker, will make. Thus, in this sense, the individual's 'freedom of choice' – in terms of deciding his own behaviour and actions – seems to be totally absent: the individual is expected to behave and choose precisely as rational-choice theory describes and prescribes. And indeed, were the individual in such a situation not to behave and choose as predicted, then the only possible and seemingly acceptable conclusion to be drawn is that the individual is not rational, if not actually irrational.

But obviously, all these conclusions follow only if all the foregoing neoclassical premises are accepted; namely, that individuals as economic agents are rational, self-interested utility-maximizers, that 'rationality' means self-interest or utility maximization, and in turn that all economic behaviour can be explained by assuming that economic agents have set and stable preferences and, subject to their constraints, make rational choices on the basis of and hence consistent with, those preferences.

Once those premises are questioned, one can then consider the possibility that individuals, even in their role as economic agents, may be motivated not only by pleasure or preference-satisfaction or self-interest, but also by altruistic or moral concerns in general; that individuals may also adopt a collective perspective, rather than a strictly individualistic one, in their socio-economic interactions; and that 'rationality' need not mean self-interest or utility maximization. As Sen (1987, p. 16) argues: 'Universal selfishness as *actuality* may well be false, but universal selfishness as a requirement of *rationality* is patently absurd.' Also, as Simon (1993) remarks: 'That economic actors desire only economic gain is a far stronger assumption than that they maximize utility. It is also empirically false' (p. 158). Indeed one can consider the possibility that utility maximization need not be the only principle on which people act – and the alternative assumption may be made, as Sugden (1982) suggests in his critique of the standard theory of philanthropic behaviour, that 'some individuals act on moral principles rather than on pure self-interest' (p. 349). Autonomous, self-determined individuals – in a true Kantian sense – can then re-emerge, with their individual freedom (and thus effective freedom of choice) properly restored to them.

1.5 SUMMARY

A view of morality as *altruism cum rationality* has been endorsed here, rejecting both the simple identification of altruism with morality and the identification of rationality with self-interest or utility maximization, as typically embodied in the economic instrumental conception of rationality.

Altruism on its own is not moral, and indeed as Alberoni and Veca (1988) argue 'altruism without reason is blind'. This can thus clearly explain the 'unfortunate' outcomes that several economists have recently claimed to be related to altruism, stressing that not only may allocative inefficiencies persist despite the existence of altruistically-motivated behaviour and resource transfers, but that altruism may even be a counterproductive social force and can actually make matters worse and everyone worse off. Also, rationality *per se* is not moral, independently of the specific formulation of rationality, and indeed 'rationality without altruism is empty'.

Moreover, human economic activity motivated by self-interest is not moral behaviour. And it is certainly not moral behaviour when individuals, in pursuing their own material self-interest, *unintentionally and unknowingly* promote the public interest, as if led by an 'invisible hand'. For individual behaviour can only be moral when the individual is responsible for his own action, and indeed the individual's *intentions* critically determine the morality of the act, and cannot hence be dismissed or ignored in a (moral) evaluation of individual conduct. Consequently, the 'fortunate' outcomes for society of an individual's self-interested behaviour – brought about by the 'invisible hand' operation – can certainly be welcomed, but cannot and should not be claimed to be proof of the morality of self-interest. The legitimacy or rationality of self-interest is not being questioned here, nor is the claim that self-interest is a natural human force. What is, however, disputed here is the *moral value* of self-interest or even of long-term enlightened self-interest.[16]

Finally, the 'invisible hand' argument, by denying the individual the possibility of moral behaviour, does implicitly deny individual effective freedom, and freedom of action and choice in particular. For genuine individual freedom – in the Kantian sense of *autonomy*, as rational self-legislation – is inextricably linked to individual moral behaviour, and hence to 'rational altruism', which in turn also means the repression and preclusion of the very calculus of one's own utility.

2 Economic, Socio-Economic and Moral-Economic Approaches to Altruism

INTRODUCTION

Economic theory has long ignored or even denied the existence of altruism, and in fact, following Adam Smith, it postulates that individual behaviour is strictly motivated by self-interest. *Homo economicus* or 'rational economic man' is, notoriously, a selfish, rational, utility maximizer who acts in isolation and lives in a Hobbesian-type state of nature.

More recently, however, and especially since Becker's pioneering works on the economics of the family (1974a, 1976a), altruism and altruistically-motivated behaviour have received growing attention. But although the admission of altruism (even if only to some extent and/or in some circumstances), and its incorporation into formal analysis, represents a clear departure from the standard 'self-interest' model, it seems to have also led to some new controversy amongst economists about the role of altruism in society and its effects on economic interactions and performance. Thus, while several studies have emphasized the beneficial impact of altruism on the family and society at large, some other works have indicated that the presence of altruism need not eliminate all social inefficiencies and can even be counterproductive and make everyone actually worse off.[1]

The present chapter does not seek to discuss all aspects of altruism relevant to economic analysis, nor is it meant as a survey of economic literature and research on (or related to) altruism. For, apart from anything else, this would clearly amount to a rather monumental task.[2]

Rather, this chapter has a much more limited scope and, specifically, two aims. The first aim is (in Section 2.1) to highlight the ways in which altruism is most commonly accounted for or modelled in economic research, as well as to emphasize the underlying assumptions about the nature of altruism and consider some important implications of those assumptions and models. The second objective is (in Section 2.2) to look at two alternative socio-economic and moral-economic approaches to altruism, at their related assumptions about the nature of altruism, and at their different implications both for economic modelling and, possibly more importantly, for social and policy actions.

Before proceeding, it seems useful to briefly summarize the prevailing views among mainstream neoclassical economists on the issue of altruism. Three views seem to be especially typical.

1. As far as private objectives and private choices are concerned – that is, in most economic behaviour – the standard 'self-interest' assumption is not only reasonable but even the most appropriate. For, in this sphere of market transactions, rational economic agents can be expected to pursue their own personal interests, and hence altruism can be safely disregarded as irrelevant. It is only (or mainly) in relation to public aims and public choices that the analysis needs somehow to take altruism and altruistic behaviour into account – clearly, in addition to the context of family behaviour.[3]

2. It is certainly true that at times individuals seem to display some degree of altruism. But, on deeper analysis, their conduct can normally be shown to be not truly altruistic, but only apparently so, and in fact consistent with (and indeed driven by) self-interest – the 'enlightened self-interest' assumption. Alternatively, the seemingly altruistic acts (such as gift-giving) can be explained in terms of self-interested motivations or egoistic incentives, such as reputation, reciprocity, social approval, status or even fear. Either way, it is on a purely individualistic calculus that individuals can be said to be ultimately acting, and altruistic preferences are hence unnecessary to explain apparently altruistic behaviour.

3. Even if some truly altruistic residual remains, after all (such as, notably, voluntary blood donation),[4] it need not require abandoning the standard economic utility-maximizing framework. For orthodox economic theory is perfectly capable of accommodating altruism, by assuming that what altruistic individuals aim to maximize is not just their own personal welfare, but also the welfare of some other person(s) they care for – leading to the concept of utility 'interdependence'.

2.1 STANDARD ECONOMIC APPROACHES TO ALTRUISM

There are two typical ways in which altruism is dealt with in economic models. (Their formal description is provided in Chapter 3, Section 3.2.)

The most common (and for many it seems the only acceptable) economic approach to altruism is 'to put it in the individual utility function'. That is, the individual *egoistic (self-regarding) preferences* – direct pleasure, 'felicity' or utility derived from own consumption – are augmented by *altruistic (other-regarding) preferences* – indirect pleasure or utility derived from another individual's utility, in turn dependent on this other person's consumption. Thus, other people's utility, well-being or consumption simply becomes an additional source of individual satisfaction (representing the individual concern, caring or 'love for others' that may in turn be genuine (pure) or paternalistic (meddlesome)), to be maximized along with own personal utility (which relates to 'self-love'). An *interdependent utility function* hence arises as either utility-related or commodity-related.

Moreover, within this approach, the *degree* (or intensity) of altruism is typically modelled by a simple preference parameter, which is assumed to lie within the unit interval so as to exclude both envy and 'excessive' altruism (the 'after-you' problem).[5] Hence depending on the actual value of the parameter, altruism can be weaker or stronger. Also, the *domain* (or extent) of altruism is allowed to be narrower or broader, both in terms of 'social' distance – with a greater weight normally assumed to be given to close family and kin than to others – and in terms of 'temporal' or 'generational' distance – with a greater weight here assumed to be attached to, for example, children rather than grandchildren, or similarly parents rather than grandparents, and hence discounting future (or previous) generations more heavily the more distant in time they are.

As to altruistic acts, such as interpersonal/intergenerational voluntary income transfers (notably bequests and gifts), following Barro (1974) and Becker (1974a), they are readily incorporated in the individual budget constraint and indeed assumed to be motivated by the individual's concern for the recipient(s) of the transfer, concern in turn modelled, as already noted, via the interdependence of the individuals' utilities.

This standard way of characterizing altruism has some important implications.

First, individual *utility maximization* is maintained as the only (and hence the proper) criterion for an individual to adopt in his own decision-making (including altruistic acts) and socio-economic interaction – altruism notwithstanding. That is, the assumption of 'maximizing behaviour' is taken to be just as valid for an altruist as for an egoist, as being indeed the only *rational* behavioural assumption.

Second, altruism is viewed as a matter of (subjective) *tastes* or *preferences*, and so, as for all tastes or preferences, has to be taken as given, as 'set' or 'stable'. Thus, altruism can be said to arise from individual instincts, impulses or passions, that is from psychological mental states in terms of pleasure or desires; or else it might be a genetic trait – with *altruistic genes* hence distinguishable from *selfish genes*.[6] And in the latter (biological) case, an individual, whether born as an egoist or an altruist, might be said to be so unconditionally, as a result of the inherited genes and to whatever extent the genes made him so.[7]

Also, and partly related to the previous points, altruism is normally assumed to be *bounded* – with the 'limits' given by the within-the-unit-interval altruism parameter –[8] and is hence implicitly regarded as a *scarce resource*.[9] Yet, altruism can in principle be unbounded; for, unlike consumption which is subject to a 'feasibility constraint', and like happiness, felicity, friendship or love, altruism is not subject to any conceivable material constraint. Moreover, like a skill, altruism may even grow with diligent 'practice', or in Hausman and McPherson's (1993) words: 'its quantity can be increased by its use'.[10] Indeed, according to Becker (1993), 'altruism may well have some of the properties of an addictive taste'; and, according to what Collard (1978) has called the Hume–Titmuss *contagion thesis*, non-selfishness may very well even have 'some of the qualities of an epidemic.' Clearly, some individuals may be capable of loving others more (that is, some may be more altruistic than others); also and as often is the case, the same individual may become more altruistic with age and experience (that is, an individual is more likely to be egoistic and self-centred as a child than as an adult). (These two possibilities can, of course, be easily handled within the conventional individual utility-maximizing framework, by for example using, respectively, a model of heterogeneous (egoistic–altruistic) individuals, and a two-period model in which the altruism parameter is assumed to differ in the two periods of individual life, being higher in adulthood than in childhood. However, it is also evident that the standard framework is less suited to deal with the possibility of an altruistic epidemic-type event.)

Last but not least, the assumption that preferences – and hence altruism – are exogenously fixed implies that they are clearly unaffected by the social-temporal context as well as, consequently, by government policies. In particular, if preferences are a pure matter of individual instincts, impulses or passions – as standard economic theory generally assumes – then very little (if anything) can be done to change them. Only some social control could possibly be exercised on them (for example, through incentive devices or punishment of selfish behaviour), beside self-control. Thus, even if the individualistic pursuit of narrow self-interest were to lead, in many situations, to less efficient outcomes, compared to a more altruistic and cooperative individual perspective, this could only be taken as a regrettable but unavoidable state of affairs, simply reflecting or confirming the essentially egoistic nature of human beings. Conversely, if preferences are (at least to some extent) determined by genetic inheritance, then, beside chance mutation, something could in theory and in practice be done to alter or manipulate them, namely through modern 'genetic engineering'. For example, if altruism were deemed to have a likely beneficial impact on group interactions, as well as a positive effect on resource allocation within the family and society, then the *altruistic gene* should presumably be developed and made more widely available throughout the population.

The other way of characterizing altruism, followed by some economists, is 'to identify it with cooperative actions'. Notably, in a Prisoner's Dilemma game, altruism thus means playing *cooperate*, while selfishness means playing *defect*. Under this latter interpretation, altruism is hence made into a *behavioural assumption*, rather than an assumption about preferences as in the former, most common, method of modelling it. Though, also in this case, an individual's altruistic-cooperative behaviour is explained in terms of the individual's own rational choice, or in terms of genetic inheritance or else cultural inheritance – by imitation of parents' or neighbours' behaviour.[11]

However, it is clear that the first approach, of entering altruism into the individual utility function, can also lead to cooperative behaviour, depending on the degree of altruism (the value of the altruism parameter), and on the subjective probability that the altruist attaches to the other(s) cooperating too (the also-called *assurance* or *trust problem*).[12] That is to say, the right combination of altruistic preferences and trust can yield cooperation, without having to assume that being an altruist means being a cooperator. In fact, altruism is neither a necessary nor a sufficient condition for cooperating, for cooperation may be prompted by some moral value other than altruism and even selfish individuals may at times (as is well known) have reasons to cooperate.[13] And, on the other hand, weak altruism may not generate cooperation even with strong positive assurance. (Likewise, as Collard (1978, p. 8) has pointed out, 'altruism is neither a necessary nor a sufficient condition for giving, for weak altruism may be Pareto-irrelevant and giving may be inspired by fear as much as love'.)

Arguably, the issue of whether altruism is an assumption about preferences or behaviour could be resolved by reference to some standard economic tenets. Specifically, the tenet that preferences are given, and individual choices arise from preferences and constraints (and expectations or beliefs under risk and uncertainty); and, following 'revealed preference' theory, that preferences are revealed in choices, or can indeed be equated with choices definitionally (provided that consistency requirements are met). Therefore, the two cited approaches to altruism could be said to be, in this way, reconciled and could be seen as somewhat equivalent, rather than alternative. However, this line of reasoning is rather controversial, and so it seems better to keep preferences and choices distinct.[14] Accordingly, altruism and altruistic motivations are also better distinguished from positive acts as well as from cooperative behaviour. Hence the former approach seems, in this respect, preferable to the latter.[15]

2.2 ALTERNATIVE SOCIO-ECONOMIC AND MORAL-ECONOMIC APPROACHES TO ALTRUISM

A first departure from the standard economic approach to altruism is to view altruism still as an assumption about preferences, but at the same time viewing preferences as *endogenous*, and hence in part at least 'shaped' by socio-cultural-political-historical factors and values, and especially by the 'close' environment – the family, the extended family and the local community.[16] According to this 'socio-economic' view, individual introspection, learning and personal experience are certainly crucial in moulding and modifying the individual's preferences. But parental education, guidance and persuasion, role models and group/peer pressure can also have a significant impact on preference formation and preference changes. And public policies (notably, education and information policies) may as well be relevant here. Thus, 'social engineering' can play some role in influencing individual preferences. In this context, altruism may be defined as a 'moral' preference, as opposed to 'hedonistic' (pleasure-driven and materialistic) preferences.[17]

A second and even more radical departure from the standard economic approach to altruism is considered here and labelled 'moral-economic'. It is to view altruism not as a matter of individual taste or preference, but rather as a *moral trait*, *attitude* or *disposition* (spontaneous, immediate and innate in all humans) that may relate to both preferences and behaviour, and that may be nurtured and encouraged or, conversely, inhibited and discouraged. As a result, altruism might grow at an individual or even societal level, or it might decline and even eventually disappear. More specifically, the view here is that altruism is a fundamental component of individual (rational) morality, alongside the other component, rationality. Indeed, altruism may be seen as an *ethical value* which together with other normative (moral or social) values – such as honesty, trust, goodwill, kindness, cooperativeness, fairness, equity, justice . . . – define an individual's ethics (the basic criteria, principles or grand rules by which the individual acts), and hence determine or influence an individual's ethical conduct or decisions. In other words, moral values significantly shape intentions or motivations of human behaviour, as well as informing individual preferences. But moral values differ from preferences (whether exogenous or endogenous), for preferences *per se* do not have a moral content or dimension. Certainly, moral values are not just subjective personality traits, and are in part endogenously determined. That is, they are neither simply the results of individual psychological mental states (like instincts, impulses, passions or emotions), nor are they merely predetermined by genetic inheritance (like human physical characteristics, such as eye colour or height). And the same social forces that are believed to affect endogenous preferences do, here, similarly play a crucial role. However, moral values are, unlike preferences, mainly the result of individual self-formation – through self-reflection and (moral) reasoning.

The distinction between preferences and moral values is, no doubt, somewhat obscured by the fact that some authors refer to values as 'meta-preferences', or else as 'second-order preferences' (as differentiated from normal 'first-order preferences'), or as 'higher-order preferences' (that is, relating to the individual's 'higher' self, as opposed to the 'lower' self).[18] Thus, according to Hirschman (1985), we may well agree with Stigler and Becker (1977) that *de gustibus non est disputandum* when focusing on 'wanton' preference changes, that is, unreflective changes in tastes; but also argue that *de valoribus est disputandum* when analysing 'non-wanton' preference changes, that is, reflective changes in meta-preferences or values. And following this line of thought, a number of authors have indeed proposed a 'bi-utility' or even a 'multiple-utility' framework, in place of the conventional unitary 'mono-utility' model. Accordingly, one individual utility function is the standard one of economic theory, based on pleasure or desire and purely driven by 'rational' self-interest (hence embodying egoistic preferences);

while the other utility function(s) is (are) driven by altruistic or some other moral concern (hence embodying moral preferences) and may thus be called 'moral' utility (utilities).[19]

Some might therefore see the differentiation between preferences (and especially moral preferences) and moral values as merely semantic. To the extent that (moral) values affect behaviour, they also affect (moral) preferences, and can thus be said to be reflected in the individual utility or preferences – such as altruistic preferences, or preferences for honesty, fairness, justice, duty, cooperativeness, and so on. Alternatively, if moral values and factors affect the individual constraints, they can be said to affect the costs, and are so implicitly taken into account. Either way, one might argue, there is no need for further or separate consideration of the individual's underlying moral values.[20]

And one might hence ask why it should matter, or make any difference, whether altruism is viewed as an individual endogenous preference or rather as a moral trait or disposition, given also that, in both cases, altruism is presumed to be shaped (to a significant extent) by the same forces or factors. The answer is that it matters to the way in which altruism is, in accordance, accounted for or modelled in theoretical analysis, since the actual method used and/or available depends precisely upon 'what' altruism is assumed to be.

In fact, it is argued here that it is only under the former assumption, namely that altruism is an endogenous preference, that the standard individual utility-maximizing framework can possibly be maintained as a feasible manner of explaining and predicting human choices and behaviour. Clearly, the assumption of the endogeneity of preferences (and hence of altruism) can 'complicate' matters very considerably in terms of the modelling exercise. As Bowles and Gintis (1993), though, note: 'Fortunately for the tractability of our models, many important problems can be convincingly analyzed without taking explicit account of the endogeneity of preference and norms. But the abstraction of endogenous preferences cannot be a general rule' (p. 99).

By contrast, if by assumption altruism is not an individual's (exogenous or endogenous) preference, but is instead regarded as a moral value, and indeed as a fundamental component of morality, then it *should not* be entered into the individual's utility function, and so individualistic utility maximization cannot formally deal with it. For morality entails the preclusion or suppression of the calculus of one's utility, and the true nature of altruism excludes any weighing of (own and others') costs and benefits. Also, treating altruism as an argument (or moral preference) of an individual's utility function may well make that individual an 'enlightened' self-interested person, but not an altruist. (It may be noticed here that not all non-egoistic concerns or motives need correspond to altruistic ones. For example, Sen (1977) proposes the distinction between altruism or 'sympathy' and 'commitment' or duty. And another possible distinction, already mentioned and generally accepted, is that between altruism and cooperativeness. Also, one may here recall Wicksteed's (1910) term of 'non-tuism' with regard to economic relations or market transactions, which he sees as a game (like chess or cricket) with its own rules, where the categories of egoism or altruism are, in his opinion, irrelevant.[21])

The essential point raised here is not whether altruism, and moral values and dispositions in general, influence and indeed promote social welfare (they certainly can); nor does it concern the related issue of the potential instrumental value (or functional justification) of moral dispositions, as means to advance individual preference-satisfaction, hence promoting the individual's objective function, and also bringing about beneficial socio-economic outcomes – an interpretation which, though, raises serious questions about the relationship between morality and rationality.[22]

Rather, the crucial issue here is whether moral values can (or should) be seen as part of the individual's 'preference system' (they arguably shouldn't). Certainly, values and preferences are interdependent, for, as already mentioned, the former significantly affect the latter. But, even if moral values were claimed to be reflected in (moral) preferences, the problem remains that individual utility maximization (although it might then still be applied) would be an inappropriate or very questionable method of analysing human choices and behaviour, when those choices and behaviour are crucially affected by moral values and concerns. As Hausman and McPherson (1993, p. 687) put it, 'even if utility maximization and morally motivated conduct are formally consistent, one might still question how *helpful* utility theory is in analyzing moral conduct.'

Thus, if altruism is viewed as a moral value, a serious problem may arise as to how economic analysis can make sense of it altogether. Such a view might, in fact, ultimately lead to the rejection of the whole edifice of orthodox neoclassical economic theory, which is built on the premise of the rational pursuit of individual 'preference satisfaction' and of economic rationality as self-interested utility maximization. And this would then result in the rejection of the standard way of modelling and solving economic problems: the maximization of an 'objective function' (utility, profit, or policy function), subject to a number of 'constraints' (individual budget, firms' costs, or government budget), yielding the economic agents' optimal choices (the individuals', firms', or governments' first-order conditions for rational choice), that is the solution to the problem.

Clearly, one might here claim that it then all turns to the empirical matter of the extent to which individual action is motivated by altruistic or other moral values or concerns; that is, to the empirical question of how relevant *action-ethic* is (as, for example, Sen (1994) refers to it). And neoclassical economists would, no doubt, maintain that, fortunately for standard economic utility theory, morally-motivated conduct is rather limited in scope – although their first, instinctive reaction would probably be that, no matter how extensive such conduct may actually be, it is in fact already incorporated into the individual's objective function, as built into the self-serving individualistic preferences. However, a large and growing body of empirical/experimental evidence suggests that, in several economic areas, individual behaviour does not conform with the standard self-interested rational maximizing model, nor is it consistent with expected utility theory, pointing instead to the seemingly crucial importance of altruism and other moral values in influencing individuals' choices and behaviour.

2.3. SUMMARY

A summary of the analysis is presented in Figure 2.1, which offers a taxonomy of altruism in relation to the main standard economic approach and the two alternative socio-economic and moral-economic approaches, underlined in turn in Sections 2.1 and 2.2 It emphasizes, for each approach, the specific underlying assumption(s) about the nature of altruism and, for each assumption, the implicit origins (roots or sources) of altruism, the consequent implications in terms of internal and/or external forces that may give rise to a change in altruism, and the related modelling methods used and/or available.

Looking at Figure 2.1, a question mark has been entered in the bottom right-hand-side corner, which corresponds to the modelling method for altruism under the assumption that altruism is a moral trait or disposition (or moral value), that is, under the 'moral-economic' approach. (Although modelling complications do also arise when altruism is assumed to be an endogenous taste or preference, that is, under the 'socio-economic' approach.)

Therefore, if one recognizes the non-preference nature of altruism and accepts instead its intrinsic moral dimension, one faces a serious

	Standard Economic Approach to Altruism		Socio-Economic Approach to Altruism	Moral-Economic Approach to Altruism
ASSUMPTION ABOUT ALTRUISM	(1) Taste or Preference			(2) Moral Trait/Attitude or Disposition (Moral Value)
	(i) Exogenous		(ii) Endogenous (Moral Preference)	
ROOTS	(a) Instincts, Impulses, Passions *ie* Psychological-Physiological States	(b) Genetic Inheritance	Socio-Politico-Historico-Environmental Forces *ie* Cultural Inheritance/ Conditioning *and* Individual Personality (partly due to genes?)	Moral Reasoning, Cultural Inheritance/ Conditioning *and* Individual Personality
CHANGE IN ALTRUISM by:				
INTERNAL FORCES	No. Only Self-Control	No. Only Chance-Mutation	Individual Learning, Experience *and* Introspection	Individual Learning, Experience *and* Introspection, *and* Moral Reasoning
EXTERNAL FORCES	No. only Social Control (*eg* Incentive Devices or Use of Punishment)	Genetic Engineering	Family, Community, Society, *and* Public Policies (*eg* Education and Inforamtion) *ie* Social Engineering	Family, Community, Society, *and* Public Policies (*eg* Education and Information) *ie* Social Engineering
ECONOMIC MODELLING METHOD	In Utility Function, *and* in Budget Constraint if preferences imply Altruistic Transfers (Bequests/Gifts)		In Utility Function(s) *and* in Budget Constraint if preferences imply Altruistic Transfers. *But* complex (and as yet mostly unresolved) interdependence with external forces	?

Figure 2.1 A Taxonomy of Altruism

challenge: to develop a new framework with which to analyse, in a more satisfying manner, individuals' choices and behaviour, as well as economic phenomena and outcomes in general. Building a new moral-economic *paradigm* is clearly an onerous task, as it involves a radical departure from the standard approach of individual utility maximization and from the traditional instrumental theory of economic rationality. And although this heavy burden might well be said to rest ultimately on the advocate(s) of such a position, this does not however mean that one should not be able (or even be entitled) to point out the serious limits of the prevailing neoclassical economic paradigm in understanding human nature and moral conduct.

3 (Non-Altruistic) Treatment of Altruism in Some Recent Economic Works

INTRODUCTION

A few recent articles dealing explicitly with altruism or altruistically-related economic issues have been selected here for investigation (and are listed in Sect. 3.1). The purpose of the present analysis is twofold. The first and preliminary aim is to review formally the two most common ways in which altruism is accounted for or modelled in current economic works, emphasizing both their underlying assumptions about the nature of altruism, and the link between the implicit premises and the conclusions drawn, that is the implications of the assumptions made and models used for the results obtained by the authors (Sect. 3.2). The second and more specific aim is to highlight, by focusing on the articles selected, three distinct aspects of the altruism debate, in an attempt to evaluate how altruism 'performs' in the literature (Sects. 3.3, 3.4 and 3.5).

The main reason behind this analysis lies in a growing sense of (personal, at least) dissatisfaction with today's common economic practice of, on the one hand, acknowledging and thus taking into consideration the existence of altruism and/or altruistically-motivated behaviour by individuals, and at the same time, on the other hand, doing so and modelling altruism in a rather questionable, potentially biased and/or misleading, manner.

The conclusions of the works are often, rather unsurprisingly, not very complimentary about altruism. Thus, some point to the not-so-beneficial or even openly counterproductive or perverse welfare effects of altruism, by purportedly showing that altruism results in softness or weakness and hence a tendency or propensity to exploitability (Sect. 3.3). Some, by seemingly interpreting altruism as a sort of *quid pro quo* (a commercial relationship, or marketplace exchange), derive the outcomes of supposedly altruistic actions as the fruit of individual strategic and enlightened self-interested 'calculus' (Sect. 3.4). Finally, some identify altruism *tout court* with cooperative behaviour, indeed with playing *cooperate* in a 'prisoner's dilemma' game, and hence, under 'normal' conditions, would suggest that altruism is more likely to be dominated by selfishness – for the 'rewards' (payoffs) for altruism are likely to be lower than for egoism, and in a one-shot game an altruist/cooperator would naturally fare worse than an egoist/defector. But by treating altruism as a genetically or culturally inherited characteristic, they suggest that evolution can sustain altruism and altruism can prevail – for those who inherit a tendency to cooperate or treat other individuals kindly are more likely than others to enjoy beneficial mutual cooperation and receive kindness in return (Sect. 3.5). However, this evolutionary treatment of altruism also raises some serious concern.

3.1 RECENT ARTICLES SELECTED

Six articles have been selected for the present analysis, with the selection based mainly on two criteria. The first and basic one is that they were all published in one distinguished journal, the *American Economic Review (AER)* or in its *Papers and Proceedings (P&P)*, except for one published in the *European Economic Review (EER)*. The second and more fundamental criterion is that they suitably cover (some in subgroups and one in isolation) the three distinct issues concerning altruism that it is here intended to discuss. The six works selected include the following (and will henceforth be referred to by the authors' initials):

1. 'Altruism within the Family Reconsidered: Do Nice Guys Finish Last?', *AER* (1988), by B. Douglas Bernheim and Oded Stark [B&S].
2. 'Altruism and the Quality of Life', *AER(P&P)* (1989), by Oded Stark [S_1].
3. 'Nonmarket Transfers and Altruism', *EER* (1993), by Oded Stark [S_2].
4. 'Uncertain Altruism and Investment in Children', *AER* (1993), by Subir Chakrabarti, William Lord, and Peter Rangazas [CLR].
5. 'How Altruism Can Prevail in an Evolutionary Environment', *AER(P&P)* (1993), by Theodore C. Bergstrom and Oded Stark [BS].
6. 'On the Evolution of Altruistic Ethical Rules for Siblings', *AER* (1995), by Theodore C. Bergstrom [B].

The pioneering works of Becker (1974a,1976a) on altruism, and particularly on its crucial role on the economics of family behaviour, represent clearly the background in this literature.[1] Indeed, all the above recent contributions can be seen as following in his steps. Some further extend Becker's altruism-in-the-family related 'positive' results, or in contrast establish some 'negative' results (the first three articles). Some focus on and expand a crucial part of his work on parental human capital investment in children, linking it to retirement support from children (the fourth). Some, lastly, pursue his socio-biological line of research on the evolution of altruism (the last two works).

The next section looks at how altruism is commonly formally treated, while the following three sections consider, in turn, three critical issues of the debate, namely: the *moral hazard* of altruism, altruism as a *quid pro quo*, and altruism as an *inherited trait.*

3.2 THE ARTICLES' MODELLING OF ALTRUISM

All the above articles model altruism in one of two ways; namely, either as an argument of an individual's utility function (described in Sect. 3.2.1), or as being equivalent to cooperative behaviour (described in Sect. 3.2.2).

3.2.1 Altruism as a 'preference' in the utility function

In the first four articles above, altruism is described and modelled, as is standard in the literature, as a subjective 'preference' in the individual 'interdependent' utility function. Specifically, an individual is assumed to have *egoistic* preferences over own consumption (from which direct utility, pleasure or 'felicity' arises), and *altruistic* preferences over another person's consumption (from which indirect utility or pleasure is derived). Moreover, altruism is typically characterized by a preference parameter, representing the relative weight attached by an individual to the utility of the other and hence reflecting the intensity or degree of altruism.

In general terms, an altruistic individual (*i*) is characterized by the following utility function (U_i):

$$U_i = u_i(c_i) + \delta u_j(c_j) \qquad (1)$$

where *j* is another individual whom *i* cares about; u_i (u_j) and c_i (c_j) are own (the other's) direct utility and consumption, respectively; and δ is the altruism parameter, with $0 < \delta < 1$ (while, clearly, $\delta = 0$ in the case of a selfish individual).[2]

In more specific terms, when utility is normalized so that individual i places a weight of $1 - \alpha_i$ on his own direct utility (or felicity) and a weight of α_i on that of the other, the altruist's utility function is given by:

$$U_i = (1 - \alpha_i)u_i(c_i) + \alpha_i u_j(c_j) \qquad (2)$$

where i = A,B and $i \neq j$; also $\alpha_i > 0$ to rule out masochism and envy (while, again, $\alpha_i = 0$ if the individual is an egoist), and $\alpha_i + \alpha_j \leq 1$ to rule out 'excessive' altruism. Here, $\alpha_i + \alpha_j = 1$ corresponds to the case of 'perfect' altruism, in which the two individuals' interests are completely harmonious, while $\alpha_i = \alpha_j = \alpha$ corresponds to 'symmetric' altruism – and hence $\alpha_i = \alpha_j = 1/2$ to 'perfect and symmetric' altruism.[3]

Three main implications follow from this characterization of altruism. First, altruism is seen as an individual's *given* preference, and indeed each individual is endowed with an exogenously determined 'fixed stock' of it. Thus, altruism is a 'scarce resource' to be economized, as it may well be worn out by use, and whose allocative implications are hence the proper focus of analysis.[4] Therefore, the possibility that an individual's own experience and behaviour, as well as the behaviour of others with whom the individual interacts, can affect or shape his own preferences is clearly ruled out. Whether an individual is an egoist or an altruist is hence simply, or essentially, a matter of individual 'taste' – and, as is well known and as also famously put by Stigler and Becker (1977), 'de gustibus non est disputandum': there is thus no point in analysing the formation (or sources) of preferences, nor can anything typically be done to change such innate tastes. Second, it is implied that the only and proper perspective for individuals to adopt in their socio-economic interactions (including altruistically-motivated actions) is 'individual maximization', firmly based moreover on preference satisfaction (with altruism being just one such preference). This hence rules out both the possibility of a collective (or team) perspective on the part of (altruistic) individuals, and that of a non (purely) preference-based individual conduct, such as behaviour based on duty, commitment or some other moral obligation or value. Third (and related), altruism takes on an instrumental role from the point of view of the 'altruist', insofar as altruism is acted upon only as a means to advance the satisfaction of the 'altruist's overall (subjective and given) preferences, that is as a means for the maximization of the 'altruist's total utility. Thus, such an 'altruist' might, in fact, be better seen as an enlightened self-interested agent, rather than as a truly altruistic individual who has a genuine concern for the interests and well-being of others and who (Kantianly) recognizes and treats others as ends in themselves, and not simply as means to the attainment of his own interests or ends.

3.2.2 Altruism as cooperative behaviour

By contrast, in the last two works altruism is identified with cooperative behaviour, and indeed in [BS] with playing *cooperate* in a prisoner's dilemma. Thus, in this context, altruism is not an assumption about preferences, but an assumption about behaviour. Although, it is argued or implied, the latter assumption can be formally derived from the former, so that altruism may be seen again as being characterized, albeit here only indirectly, as an individual subjective (and given) preference.

Specifically, under this behavioural approach, an 'altruistic' individual i is assumed to attach a weight $(1 - v)$ to his own payoff (p_i) and v to the other's payoff (p_j) – while $v = 0$ if the individual is an egoist who cares only about his own payoff. An 'altruistic' individual i thus here maximizes:

$$U_i = p_i(1 - v) + p_j v \qquad (3)$$

and, given the game's payoffs for cooperation or defection, the altruist will cooperate (even in a one-shot Prisoner's dilemma), provided that his degree of altruism (v) is strong enough. Moreover, if there is trust or assurance that the other player will also cooperate, then the degree of altruism needed for an individual to cooperate may be lower. Indeed, in an *assurance* game, as noted by Collard (1978): 'The more assurance there is, the less unselfishness is required to yield co-operation.' And by thinking of assurance as a subjective probability an individual attaches to the other actually cooperating, it is obvious that the higher the altruist's subjective probability estimate of cooperation (π), the lower the altruism required (v) for the altruist to cooperate, and *vice versa* – that is π and v can be seen as being inversely related. Finally, if both players are altruistic enough and/or trust each other enough, then mutual cooperation should clearly emerge as their dominant strategy. (See Appendix 3.1, for a more formal analysis of this issue.)

3.3 ALLOCATIVE INEFFICIENCIES, EXPLOITABILITY AND 'MORAL HAZARD' OF ALTRUISM

Among the articles selected, only [B&S] and [S_2] are largely 'negative' about altruism, in the sense of implying that altruism is likely (if not doomed) to have 'bad' (adverse or perverse) effects. After all, it should be acknowledged, their intention (and especially so in the case of the first work) is precisely that of showing that altruism 'might be a counterproductive social force' [B&S], and 'can actually make everyone worse off' [S_2]. Both these two articles seem to lead to a view of an altruist as a sort of weak or vulnerable individual, who 'may well be perceived as a "softy" and his threats may not be taken seriously' [B&S], and is thus somewhat bound to be exploited. In fact, 'altruism can increase possibilities for exploitation' [S_2], and indeed 'often entails exploitability' [B&S]. In any case, as [S_1] remarks, 'we cannot lightly assume away the possibility that altruism which is less than perfect would not invite exploitability'. And, as he adds, '(i)n this regard altruism resembles trust, forgiveness, patience, and insurance'.

More specifically, [B&S] '*merely* wish to establish the possibility that outcomes may be perverse' (italics added). Thus, whereas some previous works,[5] as [B&S] put it, '*simply* indicated that the presence of altruism need not eliminate all social inefficiencies' (italics added), in their own paper [B&S] 'take the critique of altruism as a constructive social force a step further'. In particular, [B&S] 'identify a variety of circumstances in which members of a group would actually prefer to interact with less altruistic individuals, and in which the efficiency of resource allocation is inversely related to the prevailing degree of altruism'. Their conclusion is thus, as they claim, much stronger than the previous results.

[B&S] focus in their work on situations involving two distinct types of individuals, and more precisely on the relationship between spouses. They analyse, first, the problem of the optimal choice of a partner in terms of the potential partner's degree of altruism, and then the behavioural consequences (in terms of the efficiency of the resulting allocation of resources) of selfish vs altruistic couples, where consumption is determined by strategic play.

The main result of [B&S], as summarized in their abstract, is namely that altruism need neither increase the benefits of group interactions nor improve the allocation of resources within families. Indeed, altruism: (i) can alter the social utility possibility frontier in surprising and sometimes unfortunate ways; (ii) also often entails exploitability and therefore causes family members to behave in ways that leave all parties worse off; and, in addition, (iii) altruists have difficulty enforcing agreements since they may be extremely reluctant to punish betrayals. Against such generally *negative* findings, [B&S] do also obtain one *positive* result, which demonstrates that 'sufficiently high levels of altruism almost always . . . lead to efficient resource allocations'. However and unfortunately, 'since the relationship between altruism and economic performance need not be monotonic . . ., this observation does not validate the view that altruism is generally a constructive social force'. And indeed, as they add, 'this should provide little comfort to those who subscribe to (those) traditional views'.

[S_2] similarly focuses on situations involving two individuals, and more precisely on the relationship between a father and son. The article analyses how their mutual altruism (and the specific degree of altruism) affects both their potential conflict about consumption allocations and relative utilities.

The main results of [S_2] are, altogether, not any more encouraging about the role of altruism, and may indeed be viewed as complementary to those of [B&S]. Thus, as [S_2] shows, 'mutual altruism intersected with certain initial allocations of the consumption good results in mutually agreeable transfers' – indeed autonomous, automatic (negotiation-free or conflict-free) transfers that, moreover, 'positively respond to stronger altruism'. And, in fact, '(t)he demonstration that altruism reduces transaction costs may be seen as a rationale for the persistence of nonmarket transfers'. However and unfortunately again, 'mutual altruism does not necessarily result in group (social) harmony, even though its rise narrows the conflict range. In spite of enhanced transfers prompted by such a rise, both parties may end up worse off.'[6] Thus, as [S_2] claims, '(t)hese results help explain why in some social environments a shift toward market-oriented transfers and exchanges may be quicker than in others, as the disadvantages (decline in utility) associated with intragroup altruistic linkages outweigh the advantages'.

As to [S_1], this work focuses in particular on the relationship between a family member (namely, a rural-to-urban migrant in a less developed economy) and his family, and studies how their mutual altruism can reinforce a self-enforcing agreement on remittances and support, respectively.

Most of the results of [S_1] are, unlike the previous ones, positive in nature. Thus, as [S_1] shows, and as is well known, 'the introduction of (adequate) altruism into a noncooperative game setup where selfish agents do not coordinate their (strategic) decisions can lead to improved quality of life for both agents'. Moreover, 'altruism reinforces self-enforcing agreements'; hence it 'reduces the need for costly contractual safe-guards', and thus, *ceteris paribus*, renders such self-enforcing agreements 'more cost efficient than alternative contractual arrangements'. Also, as [S_1] points out, altruism creates an effect similar to trust or loyalty, and hence 'assists the parties in solving problems that emerge when legally enforced property rights and contingent contracts cannot be written'. Several positive implications of altruism are then derived, including the likelihood that more sustainable and more mutually beneficial agreements will be formed among altruistically linked individuals, as well as in societies consisting of more altruistically linked groupings; and the possibility that 'the *general* (i.e., the non-family-specific) societal stock of altruism will rise as more familial altruism is produced'. However, this rather encouraging picture of altruism and of its beneficial role in intra-family or interpersonal relationships is somewhat abruptly dispelled in [S_1]'s final section on the 'moral hazard' of altruism, when one is critically reminded of all the possible adverse or perverse behavioural consequences of altruism.

Indeed, the altruism-related 'unhappy, second-best type of result' – common to both [B&S] and [S_2], and also highlighted in [S_1] – consists in the fact that, as [S_2] puts it, 'while an economy with substantial altruism will be Pareto superior to an economy with no altruism, an economy with a little altruism may be inferior to an economy with no altruism at all'. And as [S_2] adds, this result 'comes from the fact that altruism can increase possibilities for exploitation and limit the availability of credible [punishment] strategies, narrowing the range of possible beneficial social arrangements'. Thus, as in the 'Samaritan's dilemma', and as [B&S] show, altruism gives rise to incentive problems, with altruists compelled to undertake inefficient actions in order to pre-empt exploitation, and the more so, and hence the greater the resulting inefficiency, the stronger the altruism – what amounts to the 'moral hazard' of altruism, as referred to by [S_1].[7] Therefore, as [S_2] concludes, these results 'may explain the prevalence of economies of self-interested people rather than altruistic people', and may 'support the view that exploitation and strategic behavior nudge agents toward self-interested behavior in markets'.

More crucially, these results purportedly suggest that self-interested behaviour *is preferable* to altruistic behaviour, since, it is claimed: (i) society cannot clearly rely upon (sufficiently) high levels of altruism – which would generally (almost always) be beneficial, but are practically unattainable; (ii) 'the formation of just some altruism may not only fail to do any good but could actually make things worse' [S_1]; and (iii) in order to build up a sufficient 'societal stock' of altruism, society would quite certainly have to endure too large (and so unacceptable) welfare losses.

The (implicit) message of these works is, therefore, quite powerful. Namely, not only is self-interest a safer, more realisic (economic) preference/behavioural assumption – compared to its (largely unavailable) alternative, altruism. – but, once the behavioural consequences of self-interest vs altruism on economic performance and outcomes are carefully analysed, self-interest can also be seen as a respectable and well-deserving motivator of individual economic activity – indeed, a (morally) acceptable, if not superior, principle of human action and rationality.

In other words, these works not only provide, as intended, an understanding and plausible explanation for the existence and persistence of (allegedly) widespread selfishness and self-interested behaviour, but they seem to also provide a *justification* for it, hence (implicitly) elevating egoism as a more desirable human trait compared to altruism, and so also legitimizing it. Thus, an unfortunate (no doubt unintended) implication of these results is, quite possibly, to nurture, foster and enhance individuals' self-interest, by (indirectly at least) providing rational motivations and (moral) grounds for it.

Clearly, though, all the 'negative' results (as well as the few 'positive' ones) concerning the socio-economic effects of altruism derived in these works rest critically on the standard procedure of treating altruism as an argument (preference) in the individual's utility function, and on the specific assumptions made about the altruism parameters.

Moreover, a crucial point that seems to be normally missed from the formal analysis of these works is the reciprocal interdependence between individuals' selfish or altruistic preferences and their economic behaviour, and also between individual nature and the role of society and government, that is to say the possible (or likely) endogeneity of preferences and behaviour to the system. (To be precise, [S_1] does briefly discuss this issue, and [B&S] also briefly refer to it in their conclusions, as a potentially profitable area for future research, especially in relation to the economics of family behaviour.)

In fact, the degree of altruism and the relevance of nonmarket transfers are not only different between more developed and less developed countries (as stressed by, for example [S_2]), but are, arguably, also different between countries with 'similar' degrees of development (for example, the UK and Italy). Thus, if altruism and voluntary nonmarket transfers were to be measured in terms of, for instance:

- family integration/disintegration, in turn possibly measurable in terms of: divorce rates; proportion of single-parent families (due to separation/divorce, or due to non-marriage in the first place); proportion of children aged 16+ leaving home, and of those in their 20s still living at home;
- caring for the elderly within the family, in turn measurable in terms of the percentage of the old living on their own, or in residential/nursing homes;
- support (financial, but also emotional) within families, kin groups, and local communities, hence including charitable donations and voluntary work.

Then, presumably, one could differentiate between more 'altruistic' and more 'egoistic' societies, at similar (or different) stages of development.

And the suggestion (or belief) that socio-economic development almost necessarily results in, or is implied by, more selfishness and non-cooperative behaviour, individualism, rational self-interested calculus, materialism and even greed – a belief certainly not supported by casual observation –[8] would quite certainly not be supported by any such empirical evidence. Moreover, that belief is also patronizing, misleading and potentially positively dangerous, especially for less developed countries, for giving the impression that to be a (more) developed country means also inherently to be a country populated by (more advanced) selfish human beings.

Incidentally, a country's morality and predominant religion (for instance, Catholicism or Protestantism) can also naturally be appealed to, to 'explain' the specific findings about the 'nature' of individuals. However, morality and especially religion are often 'misused', as for instance when, starting from the subtle premise that Catholicism is a somewhat 'backward' religion, it is then inferred (implicitly or explicitly, and more typically by the Anglo-Saxon (Protestant) community) that such a religion is related to 'less developed' (more rural and backward) societies.[9] Certainly, religion plays a major role in any attempt to understand different societies' values, cultures, institutional arrangements and historical developments – and this may, moreover, be true regardless of the actual proportion of 'religious' individuals within a society. But the reason is, arguably, because, for example within Christianity, the Protestant Ethic – centred, above all, on the individual and his personal responsibility, on punishment/retribution, and on the value of work (the 'work hard' ethos) – is substantially different from the Catholic Ethic – focused more on individual solidarity and collective responsibility, on hope (as chiefly given by purification/redemption via the repentant confession of sins) and on love of life (the 'relax and enjoy yourself' ethos). And not because of a misplaced (not to say arrogant) assumption, presumption or indeed prejudice, of a 'more advanced' or 'superior' economic (if not moral) message of the former (Protestant) religion over the latter (Catholic) one.[10]

3.4. ALTRUISM AS A *QUID PRO QUO*

The article by [CLR] studies parental investment in the human capital of children, in relation to retirement support from children and parental uncertainty over the altruism of children, and also how parental investment may be affected by government intergenerational transfers towards parents, such as social security. This work does not suggest or imply the same negative (inauspicious and detrimental) consequences of altruism, as the previous works do. (Although, it should be noticed, [CLR] do acknowledge the possibility of inefficiencies 'due to 'free-riding' on the altruism of others' (referring, indeed, for such results to [B&S], first of all), and, moreover, recognize that the same phenomenon could also be observed in a slightly amended version of their own model.[11])

Nevertheless, [CLR] seem to interpret altruism as a sort of *quid pro quo*. In fact, they explicitly solve for 'the child's optimal choice of g [the gift] as a function of x [the parental human-capital expenditures on the child]'. Clearly, the higher the parental investment in the human capital (health and education) of children, the greater probably will be the children's earnings (and wealth), and hence the more likely that, holding the children's altruism constant, a gift motive (a transfer from children to parents) will be operative. However, the very idea of the parents' recognition of 'the connection between their investment [in their children's human capital] and the additional retirement support it evokes from altruistic children' – which moreover results in the parents raising their investment to the optimal efficient level, if parents are either certain about their children's altruism, or if they are uncertain, 'but are at least sure that they will receive *some* support from their children' – such an idea suggests a number of considerations.

First, if the parents' investment in the human capital of their children is, in part at least, altruistically motivated, then a clear *quid pro quo* relationship can be said to exist, on the part of the parents. Parents are altruistic toward their children, and hence invest in their human capital, but they 'expect' in return retirement support (a gift) from their children. No doubt, this might be seen by some as an example of 'reciprocal altruism'. Second, if the operativeness of the gift motive, which is clearly dependent upon children's altruism toward their parents, is made more likely by the parents' investment in the human capital of their children, then a *quid pro quo* relationship is established, on the part of the children. Children are altruistic toward their parents, and hence make a gift to them, but the probability of the gift being made is increased by the parents' own investment in their children's human capital, in the first place. Again, this might be regarded by some as a natural case of 'reciprocal altruism'.

Obviously, these relationships are nowhere near to forms of truly 'genuine' altruism. But what others are, here, possibly willing to see as 'reciprocal altruism', would (arguably) be more properly interpreted as simply private 'marketable' exchanges. Certainly, this appears to be the case for parental investment. In fact, as [CLR] quite explicitly put it themselves, 'the expectation of certain retirement support from children creates what parents perceive as an *implicit intergenerational loan* for human-capital investments beyond what parental altruism and wealth alone would yield' (italics added).[12] Indeed, and quite revealingly in this regard, [CLR] also note that 'parental altruism is not essential to any of our theoretical results' (p. 996, fn. 6), although they decide to maintain it 'because it is a realistic assumption'. In any case, 'reciprocity' may well be regarded as a non-altruistic reason for promoting the interests of others, and 'reciprocal altruism' as just a matter of 'enlightened self-interest' – with the latter being clearly *better* than strictly narrow self-interest, but also clearly *inferior* to pure altruism, from a moral perspective at least.

Moreover, it can be argued that whether or not children will support their parents when old depends much more on children's 'true' altruism, rather than on 'reciprocal' (somehow self-interested and of the *quid pro quo* variety) altruism – and this may also be true, independently of children's absolute wealth.[13] In turn, children's 'true' altruism can clearly depend on their own parents' altruism, but also on the society's culture, ethics and religion. Similarly, whether parents will invest adequately (or optimally) in their children's education may well depend much more on parents' 'true' altruism, as well as on how they value education in general, rather than on the (additional) retirement support expected in return (as a matter of 'reciprocity') from their children.

In fact, as for the degree of altruism, the value attached to education seems to be also quite different across societies, and even between countries at a 'similar' level of development (as, for example again, the UK and Italy). Thus, education can clearly be valued as a means to enhance future earnings – what might be termed as 'instrumental' education, and what seems to be the predominant or more typical Anglo-Saxon perspective. But education can also be valued as a means of 'bettering oneself', that is *per se*, independently of (or over and above) its instrumental value – arguably, a traditional perspective more typical of many Continental European and Asian countries.

A final point in relation to the work of [CLR] concerns the issue of whether 'communication' between the parent and the child can be used as a way of solving or reducing the parent's uncertainty over the child's level of altruism. [CLR] show that, in this game of incomplete information within a family, simple pre-game communication is unlikely to solve the problem, the reason being that 'asking the child to reveal his level of altruism could lead to mixed signals, since the child has an *incentive to lie* when his altruism is weak' (italics added). Therefore, as they conclude, '"cheap talk' in this case will not provide a general resolution of the uncertainty.'[14]

However, the idea of using communication as a signalling device about children types, hence to 'separate "weakly" and "strongly" altruistic children', seems to be at best naive or misplaced, and at worst cynical and deceptive, for it presupposes an understanding or belief about the nature of individuals (and, here, of parents in particular) as rather disturbing and nasty.[15] Also, the view that in this communication game, as [CLR] put it, '(c)onceivably, the child could end up lying about his true type' – and indeed the optimal strategy for the child is to 'overstate his level of altruism when the gift motive is not operative', that is, when his altruism is weak – such view (and related result) seems to reflect the usual 'free-rider' problem assumption, which in turn implicitly presupposes the self-interested, rational, utilitarian nature of human beings (and, here, of children in particular).

3.5 ALTRUISM AS A GENETICALLY OR CULTURALLY INHERITED TRAIT

Following Becker's (1976a) pioneering work on the evolutionary foundations of altruism in the family, both [BS] and [B] take an evolutionary approach to altruism – where, according to the *inclusive fitness hypothesis*, the units of evolution or replicating agents are the genes rather than the individuals.[16] In particular, by identifying altruism with playing *cooperate* in a Prisoner's dilemma (and clearly egoism with playing *defect*), [BS] show that 'paradoxically, evolution can sustain cooperative behavior between relatives or neighbors even in single-shot prisoner's dilemma models, where cooperation benefits one's opponent at a cost to oneself'. Thus, they show that 'evolution can select for altruism even in a most hostile environment' such as a prisoner's dilemma game.[17] And within the same sociobiological framework, [B] 'explores the evolutionary foundations of altruism among siblings and extends the biologists' kin-selection theory to a richer class of games between relatives', highlighting various altruistic 'ethical rules' which may enable a population of cooperators to resist invasion by mutant genes.

In [BS] '(a)n individual's strategy is determined either by genetic inheritance or by imitating the behavior of parents or neighbors', that is, cultural inheritance. By contrast, [B]'s focus is mainly on genetic evolution, where 'the objects of selection are genes rather than strategies', '(i)ndividuals do not consciously choose strategies. Instead, their actions are programmed by their genetic structure', and '(n)atural selection acts on the distribution of strategies in the population'. Though, whether through natural or cultural selection, the probability of individual survival and reproduction becomes higher, the larger the average payoff individuals receive in the games they play with their siblings, or other relatives or neighbours.

Clearly, as biologists have pointed out, if individuals were the relevant evolutionary units, and altruists were to get lower payoffs than egoists, then evolution would tend to eliminate altruists, thus providing, as [BS] note, 'a plausible evolutionary argument for selfishness'. However, if genes are instead the evolutionary units, then, as both [BS] and [B] show, altruists/cooperators may well survive and prosper at the expense of egoists/defectors, with evolution indeed selecting for altruism/cooperative behaviour, the reason being that 'both genetic and cultural inheritance are blunt instruments that typically do not operate on individuals in isolation. Those who inherit a genetic [or cultural] tendency to cooperate are more likely than others to enjoy the benefits of cooperative siblings' [BS], and are in general more likely to interact with others who share the same successful cooperative role models.[18] Therefore, both these works support the view that cooperative behaviour can persist and flourish (with a population of cooperators resisting invasion by dominant or recessive defecting mutants), and so altruism can prevail.

However, a number of points can be raised in relation to these works, and this growing 'evolutionary' literature in general.[19,20]

Firstly, and as is quite well known, in order for individuals to cooperate, altruism is not necessarily needed, and need not hence be appealed to to explain or predict cooperation. Indeed, and paraphrasing Collard (1978), altruism is neither a necessary nor a sufficient condition for cooperating, for weak altruism may not be enough and may thus be Pareto-irrelevant, and cooperation may be motivated by enlightened self-interested reasons. Also, as Collard (1978) has pointed out, cooperative behaviour may emerge under several alternative ethical systems, not all based on altruism – including the pursuit of the general will, the utilitarian outcome, the 'Kantian' principle, the Christian ethic of turning the other cheek, the Pareto principle, and the 'Rawlsian' principle.[21]

Secondly and more fundamentally, a problem with this evolutionary approach to altruism is the very idea that altruism is a genetically or culturally inherited trait, rather than being an individually chosen moral trait – indeed, a fundamental component of an individual's morality, alongside the other component, rationality.

The idea of the existence of *selfish genes* or *altruistic genes* is certainly legitimate, and so thus is a biological or economic theory based on such an assumption; but it is certainly not a universally shared or accepted view.[22] In fact, a sociobiological/evolutionary basis of altruism, which points to radical genetic reductionism, appears not only a dubious assumption – for the view that human nature and conduct can be understood and explained in genetic terms seems to be an 'escape route' for such a complex problem; but it does also seem to remove from the picture individual self-determination, free will or free choice and hence moral responsibility, by embracing a *deterministic* view of human nature and behaviour.[23] This view may clearly 'scientifically' appeal to some or even many, but it is not an ethically neutral or politically neutral view. Indeed, if individuals are what they are and do what they do simply because of what is written in their genes, because 'it is in their genes', either through chance or destiny, then there is not much scope (if any) for external (or, for that matter, even internal) factors to influence them. Hence, there is no need or reason for any collective action or government policy to try to change (even just in part) their values, behaviour or condition.[24] (Clearly, this may still leave open the debate on whether, if individuals are bad or misbehave, one should punish or in effect excuse them, depending indeed on whether genes are appealed to in blame or in mitigation.)

A similar argument applies to the view of individual altruism or egoism being *culturally determined*, by 'imitation' of 'cultural parents' or 'cultural relatives'.[25] Once again, even if there is now a recognition of the importance of the 'environment' in shaping individual preferences, values, behaviours and strategies, no room is seemingly left for individuals to develop their own moral judgement, through personal experience and reflection.[26] This is not to be interpreted as necessarily leading to the (no doubt, some may argue, potentially dangerous) view of moral 'relativism'. Rather, the possibility for moral self-determination is fundamental if individuals are to be seen as *responsible* beings. As Aaron (1994) has similarly put it, referring in turn to Schelling (1984), 'a critically important human characteristic is the capacity for self-reference through which humans judge their own lives and relationships'.

Finally, and related to the previous point, there is the issue of whether altruism can be properly understood as being simply concerned with the well-being of one's family, relatives or neighbours. For this type of altruism – which is naturally supported by the sociobiological principle of inclusive fitness maximization at the genetic level –[27] may well be seen as 'group selfishness', or individual 'enlightened self-interest', or 'ego-altruism'. The group may clearly be very small, including possibly even just one other person (son, daughter or spouse) or a few persons, or may include larger and larger numbers of people, groups or communities, arriving even at the regional or national societal level. Yet, even if so extended, such altruism is (arguably) still a self-interested 'group egoism'.[28] Altruism is here, in this evolutionary view, due to, or motivated by, or the consequence of one belonging to a particular (smaller or larger) group. Indeed, the very belonging to any such group *explains* an individual's altruism.[29] In sociobiological terms, altruistic behaviour favours the evolution of the group and so *is* a biological expression. Thus, under this interpretation or explanation, altruism has an evolutionary instrumental role or *justification*.

Certainly, natural (or cultural) evolution may select for altruism, and indeed, in the selection struggle, altruism/cooperative behaviour may favour individuals' survival and reproduction. And if so, this may clearly be welcomed.

However, 'true' altruism, in a moral sense, has to go beyond any single individual or group (no matter how large), for it has to be love for others, where the other is anyone in general and not someone in particular,[30] and has to be love *without a reason*. For if altruistic sentiments or acts can be explained, then (arguably) they are not really 'altruistic' in a moral sense. Moreover, as moral beings, individuals have to be free to be altruists or egoists, and whichever is their choice it has to be made, but not because it may be in their interest to choose to be so, but simply because it is a fundamental and *inevitable moral choice*.

APPENDIX 3.1. A 'PRISONER'S DILEMMA' WITH ALTRUISM AND/OR TRUST OR ASSURANCE

Consider a standard two-player, two-strategy symmetric game, in which a player who *cooperates* gets a Reward payoff of R if the other player also cooperates, and a Sucker payoff of S if the other defects. By contrast, a player who *defects* gets a Temptation (or free-rider's) payoff of T if the other cooperates, and a Punishment payoff of P if the other also defects. The ranking of payoffs in a Prisoner's Dilemma (PD) game is $T > R > P > S$. Accordingly, *defection* is the Nash dominant strategy for each player – that is, the best individual strategy under 'selfish' behaviour, where a player maximizes his own payoff $U_i = p_i$. Moreover, in a PD game, $2R > T + S$ so that total payoffs are maximized when both players cooperate – that is, *mutual cooperation* is the best collective strategy. But since mutual punishment is the only Nash equilibrium, this wholly non-cooperative solution is clearly a Pareto-inferior outcome.

Table 3.A1 depicts the PD's payoff matrix showing the two strategies (C, D) and related payoffs for each player, with the first payoff being that of the 'row' player (Player 1) and the second that of the 'column' player (Player 2).

Table 3.A1. The Prisoner's Dilemma

		Player 2	
		C	*D*
	C	R,R	S,T
Player 1	D	T,S	P,P

An 'altruistic' player maximizes $U_i = p_i(1 - v) + p_j v$, where v is the weight attached to the other player's payoff, p_j, and $(1 - v)$ to his own payoff, p_i. Thus, the altruistic player will here cooperate if his altruism (v) is strong enough. In particular, if he expects the other to cooperate, or, equivalently, if there is trust or assurance (a), then he will cooperate provided that:

$$R_i(1 - v) + R_j v > T_i(1 - v) + S_j v \quad \text{(A1)} \quad \text{i.e. if } v^a > (T_i - R_i)/(T_i - S_j).$$

Conversely, if he does not expect the other to cooperate, or else if there is mistrust or no assurance (na), then he will cooperate provided that:

$$S_i(1 - v) + T_j v > P_i(1 - v) + P_j v \quad \text{(A2)} \quad \text{i.e. if } v^{na} > (P_i - S_i)/(T_i - S_j).$$

In an *assurance positive* game $v^{na} > v^a$, which holds when $P_i - S_i > T_i - R_i$ – while if $v^{na} = v^a$ the game would be *assurance neutral*. Thus, with altruism and/or trust or assurance a PD game can be transformed into an 'assurance game', also known as 'trust dilemma' or 'coordination game' or 'stag hunt'. An 'altruistic' player's ranking of payoffs is here R > T > P > S, so that *defection* is no longer his dominant strategy, and indeed he has no dominant strategy: his strategy will depend on the payoff parameters and on his degree of altruism or trust. In the case of a *symmetric* assurance game, where both players have the same preferences and so their payoff ranking is the same, there are two Nash equilibria, one being the mutually cooperative Pareto-superior outcome, the other the mutual defection inferior outcome.

Table 3.A2 shows the payoff matrix for an *asymmetric* assurance game, in which Player 1 is an altruist while Player 2 is an egoist (looking at eqs. (A1) and (A2), notice that: $R_i(1 - v) + R_jv = R$, $T_i = T_j$, $S_i = S_j$, and $P_i(1 - v) + P_jv = P$):

Table 3.A2. An Asymmetric Assurance Game

		Player 2	
		C	*D*
Player 1	C	R,R	S(1 − v) + Tv,T
	D	T(1 − v) + Sv,S	P,P

Viewing the game in terms of *probability* of cooperation, if the altruistic player attaches a subjective probability (π) to the other cooperating, then he will play the cooperative strategy if:

$$[R_i(1 - v) + R_jv]\pi + [S_i(1 - v) + T_jv](1 - \pi) >$$

$$[T_i(1 - v) + S_jv]\pi + [P_i(1 - v) + P_jv](1 - \pi) \qquad (A3)$$

$$\Rightarrow \quad \pi > [(P_i - S_i) - (T_i - S_j)v]/(R_i + P_i - S_i - T_i) \quad (A4) \quad \text{or else}$$

$$\Rightarrow \quad v > [(P_i - S_i) - (R_i + P_i - S_i - T_i)\pi]/(T_i - S_j) \quad (A5)$$

Notice, in (A4): $0 \leq \pi \leq 1 \Rightarrow v^a \leq v \leq v^{na}$. In fact, if $v = 0$, so that the individual is an egoist, then π would need to be greater than 1 for him to cooperate! Whereas if $v = 1$, meaning that altruism is so extreme that the individual cares only about the other and not at all about himself, then even with a negative probability of cooperation (or certainty of defection) he would still choose to cooperate! Notice, in (A5), that if $\pi = 0$, so that the altruist expects the other to defect, then altruism would need to be sufficiently strong: $v^{na} > (P_i - S_i)/((T_i - S_j)$. Whilst if $\pi = 1$, so that the altruist believes that the other will certainly cooperate, or if he totally trusts the other or is totally assured of cooperation, then a lower degree of altruism is enough for him to cooperate: $v^a > (T_i - R_i)/((T_i - S_j)$.

Some numerical examples of an 'altruist's PD are provided in Table 3.A3. Notice that examples (1) and (3) correspond to *assurance positive* games (where

Table 3.A3. Illustrative examples of an 'Altruist''s Prisoner's Dilemma

T	R	P	S	$P-S$	$T-R$	$v^a(\pi = 1)>$	$v^{na}(\pi = 0)>$	$v(\pi)>$	$\pi(v)>$	
2	1	0	−2	2	1	1/4	1/2	$(2 - \pi)/4$	$2 - 4v$	(1)
2	1	0	−1	1	1	1/3	1/3	1/3	any	(2)
0	−2	−10	−20	10	2	1/10	1/2	$(5 - 4\pi)/10$	$(5 - 10v)/4$	(3)
12	7	4	0	4	5	5/12	1/3	$(4 + \pi)/12$	$< 12v - 4$	(4)
10	7	5	1	4	3	1/3	4/9	$(4 - \pi)/9$	$4 - 9v$	(5)
$10+\varepsilon$	10	1	$1-\varepsilon$	ε	ε	$\varepsilon/(9+2\varepsilon)$	$\varepsilon/(9+2\varepsilon)$	$\varepsilon/(9+2\varepsilon)$	any	(6)

$v^{na} > v^a$), while examples (2) and (6) correspond to *assurance neutral* games (where $v^{na} = v^a$), and example (4) to an *assurance negative* game (where $v^a > v^{na}$, so that the more assurance there is, the more altruism is required for cooperation). Also, notice that, from the perspective of a 'selfish' player who cares only about his own payoff, example (5) represents a 'risky' PD (where $T \gg R > P \gg S$), while example (6) represents a 'safe' PD (where, for ε very small, $T \approx R \gg P \approx S$) – in other words, PDs where the risk of cooperating is big and small, respectively.

Finally, it should be stressed that the 'altruistic' player's utility function may differ from the one specified here – which can be seen as a case of 'pure' altruism, and is also alternatively given as $U_i = p_i + \alpha p_j$ $(0 \leq \alpha \leq 1)$. Alternative models of altruism have indeed been suggested (see, e.g. Andreoni and Miller (1993)), all leading to cooperative play, including the model of 'reciprocal' altruism, where $U_i = p_j + \alpha$ and $\alpha \geq 0$ whenever both players cooperate and is zero otherwise; and the model of 'duty', where $U_i = p_i + \alpha$ and $\alpha \geq 0$ whenever i cooperates and is zero otherwise.

Supplement to Chapter 3 On Altruism, Fitness, Intelligence and Poverty

INTRODUCTION

For a number of decades now, and at least since the 1950s, there has been a stimulating and fruitful intercourse between economics and biology (for a recent, comprehensive coverage of such an intercourse, see, for example, Khalil (1992)). It is, however, only more recently that the full potential of such a beneficial relationship has finally emerged (and, in this respect, the *American Economic Review* should be given full credit for being a major vehicle for it).

The focus here will be on one specific area which is arguably the most relevant from the economist's perspective, namely the link between modern evolutionary theory – the neo-positivistic, neo-Darwinian genetic 'inclusive fitness' hypothesis – and the modern economic theory of altruism. In particular, as Bergstrom and Stark (1993, p. 149) believe, 'evolutionary theory can enrich the study of the economics of the family' – as Becker (1976a) clearly proved, although as Becker (1993, p. 9) also notes 'many economists dispute that altruism is important in families'.

The present work reviews the most important results so far achieved by this literature, and, by building on them, draws some additional and quite far-reaching conclusions and recommendations.

S3.1 THE ECONOMIST'S AND SOCIOBIOLOGIST'S ALTRUISM AND FITNESS

As is well known, to a professional and sound economist – whose work is firmly built on neoclassical theory, which is in turn founded on a utilitarian, rationalist, individualist, self-centred, egocentric and hedonistic paradigm – the very word *altruism* is, if not completely an aberration, certainly a painful nuisance.[1] For, as Edgeworth (1881) clearly stated: 'The first principle of economics is that every agent is actuated only by self-interest.' And for a more recent statement, Tullock's (1976) words are no less definitive, 'the average human being is about 95 per cent selfish in the narrow sense of the term'.

Altruism (unselfishness) in its pure form, if it ever exists, is obviously totally irrational, but fortunately very rare. For, as Collard (1978, p. 45) masterly put it: 'extreme forms of altruism . . . lead to absurdities'.[2] A vivid example being the 'after-you' problem, where due to excessive politeness nobody would pass through a doorway, each insisting that the other should pass first. Less extreme forms of altruism, although more acceptable, should still be discouraged. For often, as Bernheim and Stark (1988, p. 1034) lucidly explain: 'the efficiency of resource allocation is inversely related to the prevailing degree of altruism'.

Moreover, altruism is usually nothing but enlightened self-interest, or is simply based on reputation, reciprocity, reinforcement or confirmation of status, or fear. These are all rational motivations, that is, explainable and justified in terms of far-sighted self-interest, and clearly indicate that altruism is normally only apparently so or not truly so. Lastly, for those still sceptical, it needs only adding with Khalil (1992, fn. 8) that: 'A convincing argument could be made . . . that from a cognitive standpoint, altruism involves denial of legitimate self-interest which could arise, in fact, from weakness, guilt, obsession, transmuted selfishness, neurosis, and other pathologies.'

Moving on to the other side, the geneticist/biologist's perspective, the central theoretical problem of sociobiology is, as is also well known and in Wilson's (1975, p. 3) words, 'how can altruism, which by definition reduces personal fitness, possibly evolve by natural selection?'.

It is here worthwhile recalling, with Simon (1993), that in modern evolutionary theory *fitness*, the key concept, means 'the number of progeny an individual produces or, for species, the average number of progeny of members of the species'; and 'altruism means behavior that reduces the actor's fitness while enhancing the fitness of others' (p. 156). That is, as Simon (1990, p. 1665) also puts it: 'Altruism means forgoing progeny.'

Moreover, as Becker (1976a, p. 817) suggests: 'The enduring traits of human (and animal) nature presumably were genetically selected under very different physical environments and social arrangements as life on earth evolved during millions of years.' This point can also be put, more forcefully, with Poundstone (1993, p. 232): 'The genetic code allows organisms to pass on not only physical traits but behaviors. Those genetically encoded behaviors that cause individuals possessing them to survive longer or produce more offspring are likely to persist.'

Indeed, it is possible to distinguish amongst others: non-cooperative (defecting) genes and cooperative genes (see, for example, Poundstone (1993), Bergstrom and Stark (1993), and Bergstrom (1995)); genes for emotional reactivity and for emotional dependence, that is genes for social approval (see, Hollander (1990)); genes for honesty and for dishonesty, genes for intelligence and for strength (see, for example, Frank (1987, 1988, 1989) and Harrington (1989)); and finally and most relevantly here, selfish genes and altruistic genes (see, above all, Dawkins (1976)).

Thus, as Becker (1976a, p. 817) well argues: 'It is not difficult to understand why self-interest has high survival value under very different circumstances, but why should altruistic behavior, sometimes observed among animals as well as human beings, also survive?'

One solution to the problem of the survival of altruism has been the sociobiologists' appeal to 'group selection', and in particular 'kin selection', operating through the common genes of kin, where the units of evolution are genes rather than individuals. But the biologists' problem remains in that 'if individuals are the relevant evolutionary units, then evolution should be guided by selfish behavior', as Bernheim and Stark (1988, p. 1044) notice. Mercifully, a solution was ultimately found. In Samuelson's (1993, p. 143) words: 'it was with some relief that the neo-Darwinian synthesis could appeal to kin selection and 'inclusive fitness' as a basis for viable altruism in *individual* natural selection'.

S3.2 FROM ALTRUISM TO 'PAUPER HOMO ECONOMICUS'

Drawing on the existing literature, an attempt is now made to derive some logical conclusions, which, for clarity, will be formalized in a number of propositions, lemmas and corollaries. (A sketch of the analysis is provided in the Appendix.[3])

In order to establish the first result, the sociobiological definition of altruism needs briefly reviewing. As already mentioned, according to Wilson (1975, p. 3), 'altruism . . . by definition reduces personal fitness', or to clarify: 'When a person (or animal) increases the fitness of another at the expense of his own fitness, he can be said to have performed an act of *altruism*' (p. 117). Also, recalling Simon's (1993) fine synthesis: 'In evolutionary theory, altruism means behavior that reduces the actor's fitness while enhancing the fitness of others' (p. 156),

one can thus define 'altruism as sacrifice of fitness' (p. 158). Consequently, it is possible to state with confidence the following:
PROPOSITION 1. *Altruism and individual fitness are inversely related.*

The next proposition is more subtle and complex. Thus, it requires some careful 'paving', in order for it not to be received with some degree of scepticism, if not total dismay. To this aim, the works of Simon (1990, 1993) are a major source of help, besides inspiration.

Firstly, as Simon (1993, p. 157) reminds us, his (1990) 'simple model . . . demonstrates that extensive altruism will appear in populations characterized by bounded rationality and docility'. (As to bounded rationality, we can 'simply take it as an axiom: *human beings are capable only of very approximate and bounded rationality*' (p. 156). As to docility, it means: '*the tendency to depend on suggestions, recommendations, persuasion, and information obtained through social channels as a major basis for choice*' (p. 156), or more briefly, as Simon (1990, p. 1665) puts it, 'receptivity to social influence'.[4] More precisely, as Simon (1990, p. 1666) clearly explains: 'Docile persons tend to learn and believe what they perceive others in the society want them to learn and believe.'[5])

In fact, '*people exhibit a very large measure of docility*' (p. 157), and: 'Because of bounded rationality, docility contributes to the fitness of human beings in evolutionary competition' (p. 156). There is, however, a tension here, for: 'Since docile persons depend heavily on socially provided advice and orders, they often make choices that reduce their own fitness under social advice to do so. They are often unable to judge independently that a recommended choice is actually disadvantageous to them as individuals', with this being 'a necessary consequence of their bounded rationality', and they can thus sometimes be persuaded by society 'to take altruistic actions that decrease individual fitness' (p. 157). The tension inherent in docility, as far as individual fitness is concerned, is the result of conflicting advice, some fitness-enhancing, and some, recommending altruism, fitness-reducing. Fortunately, however: 'On average, [docility] contributes to [docile persons'] fitness and hence drives out non-docility in evolutionary competition' (p. 157).

Secondly, intelligence comes, finally and openly, into the picture. For 'differences in intelligence among docile individuals' have to be acknowledged. Thus, 'the more intelligent could discriminate better between advice useful to fitness and advice recommending altruism, and this difference in discrimination would extinguish altruism' (p. 157), as Stark reportedly and quite sensibly objected to Simon. However, as

Simon's (1993) new compelling model proves, 'intelligent altruists, though less altruistic than the unintelligent altruists, will be fitter than both unintelligent altruists and selfish individuals' (p. 157). In fact: 'The survival of altruism only requires that even intelligent persons cannot discriminate perfectly between fitness-enhancing and altruistic behavior', and this is luckily guaranteed by the fact that 'the boundedness of rationality is ineradicable' (p. 158). In other words, even intelligent altruists are, after all, not so intelligent, and hence altruism will survive. Therefore, the following can now be established:

PROPOSITION 2. *Altruism and intelligence are inversely related.*

It is worth noting that Propositions 1 and 2 together imply the following:

COROLLARY 1. *The more intelligent an altruist, the less altruistic, and hence the fitter.*

This is exactly what Simon has demonstrated in his (1993) model, which can therefore be used as an undisputable proof for the above propositions. However, it should be stressed here that the part of Simon's argument, according to which intelligent altruists will also be fitter than selfish individuals, is much weaker. In fact, this can be dismissed as generally false, since the cost of altruism is likely to exceed the increments in fitness for docility. Consequently, Simon's above-quoted sentence should be rephrased as follows: 'intelligent altruists, though less altruistic than the unintelligent altruists, will be fitter than them, but less fit than selfish individuals' – and, it should also be noted, independently of whether the latter are intelligent or unintelligent.[6]

Before moving on to some wider considerations, an initial implication of the above analysis can be derived:

LEMMA 1. *Childless individuals, whether infertile or not, are extremely altruistic and unintelligent.*

One might thus conclude that it is better, after all, that they do not have children. In view of its relevance, we will return to this point later.

In order to derive the next results, two sources can be quoted. First, Poundstone (1993) who writes: 'Human preferences and survival value are often quite different things. An awful lot of human preferences centers on money, which means little to survival or fertility rates. Even so, greed for money and other material things might be a side effect of genes that encourage self-interest in matters of food, water, and mates' (pp. 235–6). Second, Simon (1993) who argues that: 'fitness arguments do not imply that desire for economic gain is the dominant human motive. Perhaps in earlier centuries wealth was a major contributor to fitness . . . There is no such connection today. Population increase is generally far more rapid in the third world than in the first. Within economies like our own, there is also a negative correlation between income level and reproduction rate. The statistics show the poor to be fitter than the rich' (p. 158).

From Propositions 1 and 2 and the above quotes, it is now possible to deduce the following:

COROLLARY 2. *Third-world populations and the poor are much less altruistic and more intelligent, and hence fitter, than first-world populations and the rich.*

A question might here arise: if they are so intelligent, how is it then that they are third-world populations and poor?

It may also be noted that the 'negative correlation' between income level and reproduction rate is a confirmation of Corollary 2, in the sense that:

COROLLARY 3. *The rich are unintelligent and altruistic.*

Here, the question might be: if they are so altruistic, how is it then that they are rich?

Before attempting to answer these two crucial questions, the following is now established:

PROPOSITION 3. *Income and/or wealth and fitness are inversely related.*

The apparent paradox underlying the above questions can be solved by drawing the logical conclusion that:

COROLLARY 4. *To be rich is a sign of stupidity.*

Or, in more elegant and possibly less offensive words, a sign of bounded rationality and docility. (See the Appendix for a sketch of the analysis.)

This finding has an intuitive explanation, which is consistent with pragmatic folk wisdom, or commonsensical proverbs, such as: 'It's better to be born lucky than rich'; 'Wealth does not bring happiness'; *Divitiae curas habent comites*, that is, wealth and worries go together. All this could also be summarized by saying that it is better to be poor than rich, as it means less problems, a happier life, and, it can be argued, the joy of many children. Also, as some may add, the poor will be rewarded in the after-life, 'for theirs is the kingdom of heaven'. On the other hand, the moral of Aesop's well-known fable 'The Fox and the Grapes', in which the famished fox, at last turning away, says: 'The Grapes are sour, and not ripe as I thought', is here dismissed as clearly malicious; moreover, such a moral runs also contrary to the above conclusion that to be poor is somehow to be blessed.

Next, considering Lemma 1 and Corollary 3 together, a few additional conclusions can be drawn. Firstly, one can establish the following:

LEMMA 2. *Childless individuals should generally be rich.*

This holds quite apart from the obvious reason that they do not need to spend money on children. In fact, childless individuals' common traits are altruism and unintelligence – regardless of their heterosexual or homosexual (gay) gene, as quite recently discovered – and these are genes common to the rich. This point does also imply the following:

COROLLARY 5. *To be infertile is a sign of excessive altruism.*

Secondly, since altruism is a consequence, or a symptom, of lack of intelligence – as established in Proposition 2 – the providential mechanism of natural selection should be noticed and welcomed, as it was hinted at before. Thus, unintelligent (altruistic) individuals will be eliminated by evolution and disappear, and a pure race of intelligent (selfish) individuals will eventually emerge. That is:

LEMMA 3. *Only the intelligent, selfish, and hence fitter, individuals will survive and flourish.*

Here, Harrington's (1989) work should be mentioned, for it too suggests a clear link between intelligence and fitness: 'Individuals with greater intelligence will thrive regardless of their initial number' (p. 592).[7] (However, it should be underlined that Harrington's work – a comment to Frank (1987) – focused specifically on the survival of honesty versus dishonesty, and in that respect his central finding and major result was, contrary to Frank's, that: 'From an individual's perspective, honesty is an undesirable trait' (p. 592)).

From the above analysis, and in particular from Proposition 1, the following can now be established:

COROLLARY 6. *Fertile individuals are selfish, and the more so the higher the number of their children.*

In other words, there is a positive correlation between the degree of selfishness and the number of progeny an individual produces, that is, fitness.[8]

This is an important result, and it seems to provide support to a conviction which is rapidly gaining ground in the political arena, especially among conservatives. That is, that many extremely prolific poor people, and single mothers in particular, are extremely selfish – but quite apart from the fact that they rely and draw heavily on social security welfare benefits, hence causing higher and higher public deficits. Also, it seems to confirm the view that the poor's 'fitness' is the fruit of an intelligent, cool-minded and smart calculation, purely self-interested. Thus, individual self-interest, far from being a potentially socially harmful and disruptive force, is unarguably beneficial for humanity: with a high survival value, it also ensures human survival. Last, but not least, this result also leads to the following:

PROPOSITION 4. *The poor – selfish, rational, intelligent, utility-maxi-*

mizers (where the source of utility has to be taken axiomatically to be fitness, and not, as neoclassical economists have long and misguidedly suggested, income or wealth) – are the best, if not perfect, incarnation of 'homo economicus'.

Therefore, it is possible to conclude with the following:
POLICY RECOMMENDATION. *The smart, strong, prolific (vicious?) poor should be given the levers of power, public as well as private, for, with the help of the 'invisible hand', they would guarantee the most efficient and socially desirable outcome, also and certainly in terms of the 'survival of the fittest'.*

S3.3 CONCLUSION

Rather than attempting to summarize the analysis and all the results and policy advice which have been derived here, it seems more appropriate to conclude with a qualifying remark.

Obviously due to my genetic structure, I am both a very altruistic and childless individual (also as a member of an infertile couple). Needless to say, I must *ergo* be extremely unintelligent – almost perfectly rationally bounded and docile! This should thus explain why the present analysis may not be completely clear or convincing, or may even appear at times confusing or contradictory. Moreover and not surprisingly, this should also explain why the arguments which I have developed here seem to be in such sharp contrast with the rest of my work on this subject.

APPENDIX S3.1. A SKETCH OF THE MODEL

The main elements of the model are briefly illustrated here. First

$$\text{fn} = \text{fn}\ (\underset{-}{a}) \tag{1}$$

where fn = normal fitness coefficient, and a = degree of altruism.

$$a = a\ (\underset{-}{I}) \tag{2}$$

where I = intelligence. Putting (1) and (2) together implies:

$$\text{fn} = \text{fn}\ \big(a(\text{I})\big) \tag{3}$$

$\therefore$ as $I\uparrow$, $a\downarrow \Rightarrow fn\uparrow$

$$W = W(\underline{I}) \qquad (4)$$

where W = income/wealth; and clearly:

$$fn = fn\big(W(I)\big) \qquad (5)$$

Combining (3) and (5) yields:

$$fn = fn\big(a(I), W(I)\big) \qquad (6)$$

$\therefore$ as $I\uparrow$, $a\downarrow \Rightarrow fn\uparrow$

& as $I\uparrow$, $W\downarrow \Rightarrow fn\uparrow$

Thus, notice, the two channels through which intelligence positively affects fitness reinforce each other.

4 Ethical and Political Non-Neutrality of Neoclassical Economics*

INTRODUCTION

The mainstream of modern economic theory is built upon two crucial assumptions, namely that (i) tastes are given, and (ii) individuals are rational, self-interested economic beings. An important, additional assumption normally made in the economic literature is that of 'Nash conjectures', that is each individual, when deciding his own utility-maximizing action, takes the behaviour of everyone else as given.

Selfishness and independent (isolated) behaviour are the critical premises for the 'free-rider' problem and the resulting private underprovision of public goods and philanthropic-charitable activities; and for the 'prisoners' dilemma' and 'isolation paradox' (Sen (1967)) which lead to non-cooperative inferior outcomes.

However, the widely observed examples of apparently non-selfish motivations, and the empirical extent of voluntary cooperation seem to be in marked contrast to, and inconsistent with, standard theory. Consequently, several studies have directly addressed the issues of altruism and cooperation, and they fall broadly into one of the two following categories. First, studies which attempt to explain, on the one hand, seemingly altruistic feelings in terms of self-interest, even when this requires engaging in *ad hoc* theorizing; and, on the other, spontaneous cooperative outcomes as very special cases due to particularly favourable circumstances. Second, studies which take a more radical stand, and to a greater or lesser extent depart from conventional economic theory, by 'accepting' that altruism and voluntary cooperation are more or less common phenomena, and hence amending, if not reversing, basic economic postulates. Thus, a number of studies provide 'rational' explanations of spontaneous cooperative behaviour, against the 'rationally' expected non-cooperative one.[1]

In spite of a growing and by now quite large literature on this issue, there still seems to be, however, some confusion about the two separate, though possibly interdependent, themes of selfishness vs altruism and non-cooperation vs cooperation. Thus, before proceeding any further, a few clarifications seem to be in order.

Firstly, in *standard terms*, selfishness or altruism are a matter of tastes or preferences, and are thus represented in the individual utility function. (More precisely, a selfish individual cares only about his own welfare. Conversely, an altruistic individual cares also about other people's well-being; here, 'genuine' altruism would indicate a general concern for someone else's welfare, whereas 'paternalistic' or 'meddlesome' altruism would indicate a specific concern for other people's consumption of some goods (for example, merit goods).) Non-cooperation or cooperation are, on the other hand, a behavioural matter, and are therefore related to the manner in which individuals decide their own actions. (In particular, a non-cooperative (atomistic) individual assumes that his actions are independent of others'; whilst a cooperative individual assumes an economic interdependence between his and other peoples' actions, and collaborates with others.)[2] Secondly, it is held here, non-selfishness, or else altruism, is neither a necessary nor sufficient condition to generate spontaneous cooperative behaviour, although it can facilitate it. Thirdly, it is also held here, not only can preferences and behaviour be interrelated, they can also be endogenous to the system.

The main purpose of this analysis is not so much to question the central assumption of neoclassical economic theory, that is to say 'rational self-interest', but rather to question its presumed ethical neutrality.

Indeed, one implication of the presumed moral neutrality of the 'rational self-interest' assumption is an implicit 'right-wing' bias in economic theory. (Thus, private is good, public is bad, or, private are the virtues, public the vices. Competition is healthy, cooperation is not feasible. Economics can only properly deal with the problem of resource allocation (efficiency), and not distribution (equity), as the latter entails some moral criterion which lies outside the sphere of economics.)

In fact, the assumption of exogenously given tastes, and of individual optimal choices as the outcome of objective constraints, relates to the basic ideological distinction between 'Left' and 'Right' with respect to 'human nature', and implicitly takes the latter view. Broadly speaking, and according to the traditional interpretation, the Right's view in this respect is that genetics is more important than the environment in determining human nature, while the Left's is the opposite. Thus, the Left's position stresses the endogeneity of preferences and behaviour.

After all, the Father of modern economic theory, Adam Smith, formed his doctrine at the British Right-wing philosophical school of Hutcheson and Hume, under the influence of Hobbes and Mandeville.

The conviction, which may be conscious or unconscious, that economics – likewise sociology, psychology, psychoanalysis, politics – is a discipline independent of ethics, or else that they are two different and separate 'categories', is certainly a legitimately tenable one. However, it reflects a very specific philosophical stand, and is by no means unanimously accepted, nor is it in any sense 'neutral'.

More precisely, classical economic theory is, from a philosophical point of view, a teleological ethical theory, according to which acts have only an instrumental value, while it is the consequences of those acts which have an intrinsic value. In other words, actions have to be judged by their results, and the moral motivation of the acts is somehow irrelevant. Thus, this theory is philosophically in contrast to a deontological ethical theory, which attributes intrinsic value to features of the act themselves. To use some examples, the former theory would consider an altruistically-motivated action, but which results in an unfortunate outcome, as not praiseworthy. By contrast, the latter theory would regard 'lying' as wrong even if it produced better consequences than the alternative, 'telling the truth'.

Similarly, the conviction that economics is a technical/scientific discipline, which yields 'objective' results, is a by-product of the conviction that the basic postulates on which it is built are morally neutral. Holding such convictions can certainly be more reassuring or less disturbing, both for economists as well as, and possibly even more, for non economists; however, and no matter how appealing, this is not a sufficient reason for not questioning the very nature of these convictions.

The fact that these convictions are, nevertheless, widely held among economists has certainly much to do with the Father's own view. At the same time, a significant part of the explanation may also lie in the fact that economics, in more recent times, has been largely dominated by Anglo-American Schools and Journals, where Adam Smith's tradition is most ingrained. Moreover, due to a highly specialized educational system, most Anglo-American scholars of economics are normally not 'exposed' to Philosophy, or Sociology, Anthropology, Politics, Law or any other economic-related social discipline. Thus, their lack of such knowledge may have contributed to their keen, and often unquestioned, acceptance of presumed-to-be neutral postulates.

Therefore, to question and challenge the basic assumption of standard economic theory – the rational selfish utilitarian nature of *homo economicus* – is not only legitimate from an empirical viewpoint, on account of the extensive evidence of altruism and cooperative behaviour.

It is also theoretically legitimate, given standard theory's morally non-neutral, and *de facto* right-wing biased, nature.

Consequently, the 'reverse' postulate, of an altruistic and voluntarily cooperative man, who may be called *homo ethicaus*, should be given at least equal consideration as the 'normal' postulate. This reverse postulate would, clearly, shift the ideological bias in economics to the Left, with several important implications for economic theory and policy; and it could be the basis for a new, Left, economic theory, parallel to and coexisting with the old, Right, one.

4.1 SOME THOUGHTS ON THE 'PRISONERS' DILEMMA' AND 'FREE-RIDER' PROBLEM

A legitimate dissatisfaction with standard 'tenets' of neoclassical economics, both on theoretical and empirical grounds, arises from the 'Prisoners' dilemma' and 'free-rider' problem. Firstly, the 'Prisoners' dilemma' points to a contradiction of the 'rational, self-interested individual' postulate. If cooperation brings about a superior outcome for everybody, then intelligent, well-informed, rational individuals would, as they should, all choose it. It is only by suggesting that the true individual nature is egoistic, greedy, and prone to cheat that the problem – Prisoners' dilemma/Isolation Paradox, where, in game theory terminology, the 'temptation' payoff strategy is followed – arises, in theory in the first place as well as in practice. In fact, this can be seen as an instance of self-fulfilling prophecy, which relates to the empiricist methodology, where the postulates of selfishness and non-cooperative behaviour are taken as facts. In practice, messages and signals may play an important role in forging that very same human nature, which is claimed to be exogenously given as such. Therefore, maintaining the assumption of individual selfishness and (Nash) non-cooperative behaviour suggests *either* individual 'irrationality' or myopia *or else* stubbornness on the part of the theoretical and/or empirical economist. This is why, given the conspicuous evidence of spontaneous cooperation, several explanations of it have been put forward, though mainly in an attempt at reconciliation with, and extension of standard theory.

Secondly, the well-known and related 'free-rider' problem – which points to the failure of private voluntary cooperation in the provision of public goods, thus providing a rationale for collective provision – is, similarly, the fruit of the 'rational, selfish, utilitarian and atomistic individual nature' assumption. Tax evasion can be clearly interpreted as an instance of free-riding, where rational individualists avoid their share of the cost of public expenditures, while still enjoying the benefits. Thus, according to standard economic theory, a society with a larger number of tax evaders should be populated by more selfish individuals, than a society with fewer tax evaders; and, as a result, it could be argued, the former society should also exhibit a smaller share of public expenditure over GDP. Moreover, the extension of the free-rider problem to the political arena would suggest that the more individualistic society should have a smaller voting turnout. However, such economic and political predictions do not seem to be confirmed by the evidence of countries showing very different degrees of tax evasion. For example, in a comparison between Italy and the UK, Italy undoubtedly has a much higher tax evasion problem, but also a higher public spending/GDP ratio, and unquestionably a much higher, and very high in absolute terms, electoral turnout. Furthermore, the rational individualistic assumption at the basis of the free-rider problem appears to contrast with the seemingly highly family-oriented and highly politicized nature of Italians.

Therefore, either *ad hoc* explanations are given of why, within a society, the free-rider problem shows itself in some instances and not in others, or, and preferably, some alternative theory, able to account in a consistent way for the seemingly contradictory evidence, is developed. If such an alternative theory were to be based on the 'reverse' postulate of altruistic and cooperative individuals, then the problem of accounting for different degrees of tax evasion across societies might, for example, be explained in terms of different societal degrees of individuals' satisfaction with public spending efficiency and efficacy, rather than in terms of degrees of individual rational selfishness.

4.2 ON THE ETHICAL NON-NEUTRALITY OF THE 'SELFISHNESS' ASSUMPTION

The presumption that selfishness is a morally 'neutral' assumption, as Collard (1978) argues, is based on the view that, on a continuous scale ranging from envy, malevolence or hatred to sympathy, benevolence or love, self-interest lies in the middle.

This position is however indefensible, once it is recognized that selfishness is synonymous with 'egoism', a Latin word meaning 'exclusive love for oneself', as opposed to its contrary, 'altruism', also a Latin-derived word meaning 'love for others'.[3] That is to say, etymologically, egoism and altruism are antithetical terms lying at two opposite extremes, though each may certainly be present in different degrees. In other words, an altruist may only be weakly so, or he may be a perfect altruist; and similarly for an egoist.

In contrast, envy, malevolence or hatred on the one hand, and sympathy, benevolence or love on the other, are concepts completely distinct from egoism and altruism. They all refer to specific sentiments and inclinations towards others, or oneself. Here, the middle assumption in relation to others would be indifference or apathy, a Greek word meaning 'lack of passion or sentiment'. Thus, the fact that I neither hate nor love other people does surely imply that I am indifferent toward them; but it does not necessarily imply that I am selfish, as I might even hate myself. At times, the hatred-to-love feelings may represent the motivation, or one of the motivations, for either egoism or altruism; but they do not lie on the same scale as egoism and altruism.

The point made here is not to deny the possibility, or even the likelihood, of man being selfish. What is argued here is that selfishness is, certainly, a non-neutral concept or assumption. Thus, selfishness is an ideologically legitimate assumption, but so is its opposite, altruism.

4.3 SOME IMPLICATIONS

Recognizing and accepting the ethical non-neutrality of standard economic theory's basic assumptions about human nature – that individual tastes are given, and *homo economicus* is a rational, selfish, utility-maximizing, non-cooperative person – and their implicit 'right-wing' bias, is conducive to several important observations and implications for economic analysis and policy.

1. The two alternative postulates on human nature – the 'normal' one of a rational, self-interested, non-cooperative individual, and the 'reverse' one of a rational, altruistic, cooperative man – should be regarded as equally plausible.

Consequently, parallel to the 'old' and right-wing biased economic theory, built upon the 'normal' postulate, a 'new' and left-wing biased theory, based on the 'reverse' postulate, would coexist with similar legitimacy.

2. Human nature in terms of objectives and behaviour, that is, whether selfish or altruistic and whether non-cooperative or cooperative, may differ across individuals and societies; and it may also differ across

time periods and generations. Thus, different societies may exhibit different degrees of homogeneity in individual nature at any particular time; and, over time, their relative degrees of homogeneity might be reversed.

An important implication of this observation relates to the formalization and choice of government policies, as well as the coordination of international policies. More precisely, when choosing among possible policies, a government has to make specific assumptions about individuals' nature, both concerning individual preferences and individual behaviour and hence expected reactions to policies. In other words, the selection of policies is based on government's guesses about the 'true' human nature. Thus, the possibility of actual misperception or misjudgment of individuals on the part of the government cannot be ruled out. Clearly, if this were the case, the government would be following the 'wrong' policies, which would lead to inefficient outcomes.

Similarly, an efficient and successful international policy coordination requires a correct knowledge by the governments involved of their own societies and of the other societies. Obviously, the chance of a national government misjudging the 'nature' of foreigners seems even higher than that of its misjudging the 'nature' of its own citizens. Hence this enhances the probability of 'incorrect' international policy formulation and implementation.

3. The basic ideological distinction between Left and Right, with respect to human nature, is not only reflected in a more 'optimistic' conviction by the Left about individual altruism and social cooperative behaviour. It is also reflected in the different weights attached to genetics and environment in the very determination of human nature, with the Left broadly believing in the environment as the more important determinant, while the Right in genetics.

Therefore, the 'normal' classical assumption that tastes are 'given' is a logically natural 'corollary' of the Right's position, and not an ideologically, and morally, neutral view.

Another important implication of this consideration is that the new, Left, theory would be characterized not only by a more 'positive' belief in human nature, but also by the belief that the society as a whole, and government policies may play a significant role in forming individuals' characters, and in inducing changes in individual preferences and behaviour, by means, for example, of information and education policies. In other words, this alternative theory would not take individual and societal degree of altruism and cooperative behaviour as exogenous, but would recognize their endogeneity to the system.

4. The previous observations suggest an alternative and, arguably,

and indeed on their mutual independence as separate categories, has also led to a view, that of 'political realism', according to which politics lies outside morality, and cannot be judged in moral terms and with moral criteria. This conception, which may be traced back to Machiavelli, sees politics implictly as a struggle for power and the exercise of power and authority – rather than as pure and diligent care in the administration of the *res publica*, or public good, in the interest and for the well-being of all individuals in society. Hence, it is claimed, the aims of politics, the means used to achieve those political aims, and the politician who exercises political power and choices, have all to be judged with different and separate criteria – political criteria, based on the rules of politics and the nature of the political game, and according to the doctrine of power and the realism of power in politics.

Similarly, it is claimed, economics is a separate sphere from ethics, religion and politics, and should be similarly defended from inappropriate and undesirable interference from ethics and religion. Thus, economic aims and means cannot and should not be judged in moral terms, and indeed economic aims justify all means used to achieve them. The maximization of profit and of personal utility are the accepted, economic proper aims, for firms and individuals respectively, and these are thus the aims that economic agents *ought* to pursue. Therefore, any means, no matter how seemingly distasteful or ignoble, can and should be 'rationally' used in this legitimate economic pursuit, provided only that it is a legal means – that is, provided only that economic agents *play by the rules of the game*, as notably argued by Friedman (1962).

The potential or even actual damages to society of this conception of economics as a separate and autonomous category, with its own logic and rules independent of ethics, cannot, however, be undervalued and may certainly be quite significant. In fact, such a view can legitimize or indeed foster individuals' economic behaviours and activities which, although not strictly illegal, are hardly distinguishable from deception, fraud or corruption in general, and which may well connive with illegal conducts.[2] Thus, the ultimate harm to society of this position may be far greater than its original benign intent of protecting economic (as well as political) aims and activities from the unreasonable and intolerant hindrance of religious and moral purists. For on this common view, morality, instead of representing the ultimate criterion of judgement for everything, is generally relegated to the sphere of human solidarity, love, altruism and generosity.

However, to defend the pluralism of values, against the claim of their universality and temporal stability, does not necessarily entail supporting such a position – namely, that of the independence of politics (political realism) and of economics from ethics. On the contrary, as the above-mentioned moral thinkers argue, since the moral philosophies of 'truth' have today rightly lost the credit that was previously placed on them, it is now not only possible but indeed fundamental to sustain once more the primacy of ethics over politics and economics. Accordingly, it can be argued, everything and every action and value, economic and political ones included, can and should be morally judged.

As to economics in particular, the moral judgement should, moreover, apply with respect to both economic research and teaching – a 'moral' economist can, no doubt, presently face some 'moral dilemmas' in both these areas of his work (discussed in Sections 5.1 and 5.2, respectively); as well as with respect to economic forecasting (Section 5.3). Likewise, economic terminology and the very use of economic concepts should be scrutinized and morally assessed, in view of the significant impact that these may have on many individuals' lives, and on the economy and society in general (Section 5.4).

5.1 ECONOMIC RESEARCH

Looking at more recent economic research from an ethical perspective, one may suggest that there is an urgent need to redirect research work amongst economists toward 'purposeful' lines. Several arguments can be put forward to support such a position.

First, there has been a clearly questionable progressive 'scientification' of economics, and a move toward an 'extreme' version of formal analysis (that is, mathematization/modelling), as if even rather trivial points could become serious, provided only that such points are properly modelled with analytical elegance – a mathematical/formal model is, in fact, naturally 'expected' as a supposedly necessary element of any worthy paper. All this, moreover, implying the quite laughable outcome that often, if not in most cases, pages and pages of highly sophisticated mathematical calculations and manipulations of equations result in 'proving' nothing more than some obvious or even quite banal point: if only 'common sense' had been used to start with, a simple sentence or proposition would have been all that was needed to make the point. (As an example, and one that is not totally removed from some real ones, the following may be considered: It is better to have a beautiful, intelligent and rich wife, than an ugly, stupid and poor one!)[3]

Also, economic research articles seem to frequently suffer from one or more of the following 'defects'.

- Their relevance is negligible (lacking any sensible purpose), and it is so not only in a possibly 'objective' sense, but also in the seemingly unashamed intention of the author. Research work, that is, is interpreted as a 'game', enjoyable, even if tiresome, but nothing but a game, and can hence degenerate into empty formal exercises.
- The analysis is potentially positively 'dangerous': by building on standard neoclassical selfish/uncooperative assumptions, the models' results may support or suggest 'nasty' conclusions.[4]
- Their expected readership is only an 'internal' one: that is, there is no evident intention to make the work more understandable to a wider audience, and indeed there appears to be a deliberate effort to make it unintelligible to such an audience, as if the latter should not, after all, try to understand or interfere in a 'private' matter. There is, in other words, a transparent aspiration or objective to make themselves accessible only to a small elite of similarly highly trained 'professional' economists, who no doubt can fully appreciate such an 'in-code' work.
- The analysis displays an ever increasing reliance on other sciences (especially evolutionary biology and physics, besides, of course, mathematics) and/or particular psychological or (moral) philosophical theories, conveniently selected so as to formalize and justify economic 'anomalies' – as, for example, 'prisoner's dilemma' or 'free-rider problem' cooperative solutions; more generally, to overcome deficiencies in standard neoclassical theory, and above all to give supposedly scientific foundations to whatever points the authors wish to make (which would otherwise remain unsupported claims).

Moreover, a paradox here is that more and more research works address not strictly economic issues – but socio-cultural, psychological, anthropological, political, religious ones, which had been originally carefully and explicitly outstripped from the area proper of economic investigation – and, more importantly, they do so with pure economic tools and techniques, often completely inappropriate or inadequate for such an investigation. Hence, not surprisingly, this frequently yields rather 'unconventional' (often plainly nonsensical) neoclassical-oriented results, which become, however, accepted as fitting quite 'nicely' within the edifice of orthodox economic theory. This is, of course, the so-called phenomenon of 'economic imperialism', which is an ever growing tendency ranging from the economics of the family, of religion, of crime and punishment, of education, health, sex, fertility, sport, diet, art, environment, . . ., to heaven and hell.[5] After all, the predominant view seems to be, economics is only a 'box of tools', which can thus be used for whatever purpose, if only applied in a proper/correct manner. Therefore, having formally made itself into a 'science', by purifying itself of any contaminant/contagious virus, economics is now, as a 'science', able and clearly entitled, according to the dominant view, to tackle any topic and subject area.

A potential, genuine moral dilemma in economic research topics and directions does thus emerge. For not only are there no evident incentives to undertake 'different' or non-mainstream research, but there seem to be, on the contrary, clear in-built disincentives, especially in terms of expected audience and publication prospects in 'core' journals, with any unorthodox work being allegedly a-scientific and hence unworthy.[6] Therefore, a 'moral' economic researcher may well feel as if left with no choice, no matter how strong the demands of his morality.

5.2 ECONOMIC TEACHING

Turning to a moral evaluation of economic teaching, it can safely be argued, for it is a generally undisputed view, that economics textbooks have a strong 'bias' toward the 'neoclassical paradigm': a rationalist, individualist, utilitarian, hedonistic, teleological, ethical philosophy. Such an overriding neoclassical bias is firmly ingrained, in the texts, in:

- the characterization of *homo economicus*, as a self-interested, rational, utility-maximizing, unemotional and coolly calculating human being, who moreover derives utility or satisfaction only (or mainly) from consumption of goods and services and from leisure;
- the assumption that individual preferences are given, as set and stable, with no attempt being made to explain how they are formed, and why and how they can change;
- the assumption that the individual (consumer/producer) is the decision-making unit – each individual acting independently and non-cooperatively, and indeed atomistically pursuing his own (narrow) self-interest – and that society is simply and only the sum of individuals;
- the tenet that economic acts are not to be morally judged: according to the accepted 'means-end' scheme, acts/means are rationally selected to realize goals/ends, and their selection is purely based on positive

(rational, logical/empirical) grounds, and not on normative (ethical/ prescriptive, value-judgemental) grounds;
- the emphatic distinction between positive and normative analysis, with the innuendo that economics is, as a science, a positive discipline.

However, and albeit common, this theoretical framework gives rise to several highly controversial and contestable explanations and predictions of economic phenomena, behaviours and outcomes, particularly in microeconomics and in the public choice literature, but also in macroeconomics. Some, most notable, examples include the following:

- Game Theory analysis, where individual Cheating or Betrayal are to be expected → Need of Pre-Commitment Devices, Legally Enforceable Binding Agreements, (Credible) Punishments, Sanctions, or (Material) Incentives, in order to get Compliance Behaviour. In particular:
  - Prisoner's Dilemma → Non-Cooperation as the Dominant Nash Strategy, with the typical example of Oligopoly → Collusion/Cartels.
  - Free-Rider Problem → Private Under-Provision of the Public Good, and also traditional utilitarian Explanations of Voting Behaviour/ Charitable Giving/Tax Evasion.
- Externalities, with the emphasis on Individual Private Costs/Benefits versus Social Costs/Benefits → Need of Market Mechanisms rather than Moral Behaviour.
- Firms' Profit Maximization as the only (overarching) proper and relevant goal – likewise Individuals' Utility Maximization.
- Altruism as irrelevant, uncommon, insignificant, very limited in scope → Ignore it, or put it in the Utility Function, or reinterpret it in terms of Selfishness of some sort → Not Truly Altruism, only apparently so.
- Leisure as increasing Utility → Work as decreasing Utility/providing Disutility.
- Public Choice explanation of Governments' Goals → Maximize Votes, and likewise explanation of Bureaucrats' Goals → Maximize Power.
- Political-Economic Models of Government Policies, where Different Governments have Different Utility Functions → No Party Ideological/Ethical Distinction.
- Efficiency/Allocation of Resources as the main, if not the only, criterion of Economic Valuation → Equity/Distribution of Resources mostly ignored → 'Income Distribution' problem, 'Fairness' and 'Social Justice' considerations left to Politicians.
- Idealized view of Competitive, Unregulated, Free Markets, as capable of achieving, with the providential help of the *Invisible Hand*,

an Efficient, and hence Socially Desirable, Economic Outcome → Negatively-biased view of State/Government Intervention, not only as not required (for free markets, if only not interfered with, will eventually lead to an optimum competitive equilibrium solution), but also as likely to be harmful → the 'more harm than good' philosophy (or dogma) in relation to any government intervention in the economy.

Indeed, the textbooks' predominant neoclassical bias has quite relevant implications. Firstly, and as already mentioned, it entails a biased (hence not universally agreeable or accepted) understanding or explanation of economics, of economic issues and problems, and of economic agents' values and behaviour. And in fact, each of the basic assumptions of neoclassical economic theory can be legitimately questioned, both in economic and moral terms.[7] Secondly, and possibly most importantly, it involves a non-neutral, but very specific and powerful 'influence' on economics students. Unless students are well equipped with a strong critical, ethical-philosophical 'knowledge', the likely result is that of 'forging' human beings who will closely reflect *homo economicus*' characteristics. The bias thus implies a serious risk of 'producing' deceptive, devious, unscrupulous, totally selfish, antisocial/asocial, immoral/amoral, greedy and vicious individuals. Evidence of such an influence is provided by several studies that, based on laboratory experimental tests or surveys, compare economics and non-economics students. These studies generally support the hypothesis that economists are different and that studying economics does encourage self-interested behaviour and tends to inhibit cooperation.[8] In turn, this points to the possibility or likelihood that, as economics graduates enter several different professions, there may well be a strong impact on how these areas will perform – according, that is, to strict standard neoclassical economic principles. Such performance can then be used as evidence to prove that economic agents behave, after all, as the theory of *homo economicus* suggests, hence realizing a self-fulfilling expectation. Clearly, a 'vicious' or 'virtuous' circle can be claimed to exist, depending on personal value-judgement.

A moral dilemma for a 'moral' lecturer of economics does thus arise and may be described in terms of the following two questions. First, to what extent should the general assumptions of mainstream neoclassical economic theory be discussed and counter-argued during lectures, and the (ethical and political) biases exposed? For the potential risk of doing so is that of 'confusing' and undermining basic economics

whether it is a genuinely definitional matter or an assumption, as for (3) and even (1) and (7). However, both definitional and behavioural examples reflect a 'commitment' to a particular philosophical/ideological/political theory – more precisely, to what has been referred to as the *neoclassical paradigm*, rooted in the utilitarian ethics and in the social (liberal/conservative) philosophy of radical individualism. Such a commitment may certainly be unconscious, with the economist, that is, lacking awareness of it; or else it can be conscious, albeit possibly undeclared.

But why, one might ask here, should all this matter? Could it not be, after all, just (or mainly) a semantic issue?[11] To emphasize that this is not the case and that all this matters, three main implications can be considered (alongside those already underlined in Section 5.2).

Firstly, and as previously stressed, the ability of standard neoclassical economic theory to properly understand, and hence explain and predict, economic phenomena, outcomes and behaviours may be limited, if not totally undermined by its very assumptions and definitions. This is, of course, particularly evident when economic matters are viewed from the perspective of someone who does not subscribe to the neoclassical paradigm and so disagrees with, regarding as seriously inadequate and even misleading, those definitions and/or assumptions. Moreover, this also leads to the economist's 'keen' reliance on psychological (emotive) and/or biological (evolutionary-genetical) factors and theories, in order to account for otherwise unexplainable outcomes or conducts, rather than having to 'revise' the philosophical/ideological/political foundations on which the theory and its definitions and assumptions are based upon.

Secondly, the use of language or terminology and concepts, likewise any specific examples provided in the economic textbooks (as similarly the examples given both verbally and practically in real life), do influence people – indeed, not only students, but also the 'man in the street', and politicians and decision-makers in general (for example, businessmen, taxpayers, consumers). Therefore, a particular philosophy, ideology, or political theory can be 'legitimized' and more likely propagated.

Thirdly and related to the previous point, decisions may be (and often are) made accordingly, with 'real' economic effects occurring to individuals and society as a whole – where the effects may well be undesirable, if not detrimental. Three examples can be given here. First, individuals and firms may end up following game-theoretic recommendations, prescribing the dominant Nash non-cooperative strategy as the 'rational' optimal behaviour, although this clearly leads to a suboptimal individual and collective outcome. Second, governments may end up (as in more recent years) dismantling both public (state) education and national health services in favour of allegedly more efficient private education and superior private health care, as well as dismantling existing national (state) pension schemes in favour of also allegedly superior private pension schemes. Here, a clear presumption is being made, concerning the private sector's ability to deliver better services than the public sector does, based on mainstream economic theory's 'results' (turned into indoctrination or dogmas), while considerations of equity, fairness, justice and other moral values are totally ignored, if not openly dismissed. Third, and more generally, governments may embark (as again in more recent years) on vast privatization programmes of state enterprises (including public utilities), and extensive deregulation of labour markets. Here, the credo is that of the *laissez-faire* economy, according to which competitive, unregulated/deregulated free markets are axiomatically more efficient in achieving economic outcomes, than a mixed economy with regulated markets and a more-than-minimal role for the government.[12]

Supplement to Chapter 5
Is the 'Dismal Science' a Corrupting One As Well?

INTRODUCTION

In a recent paper suggestively entitled 'Does Studying Economics Inhibit Cooperation?', Frank, Gilovich and Regan (1993) provide additional evidence in support of the hypothesis that economists are different:[1] they are more self-interested and more likely than others to free-ride. Also and perhaps more importantly, the authors provide some preliminary evidence that studying economics does in fact encourage self-interested behaviour and tends to inhibit cooperation.

Faced with this evidence, most economists are typically highly sceptical, questioning its very reliability, if not altogether unconcerned, dismissing or even ignoring the issue as a non-relevant one. Indeed, the fact that, as Hausman and McPherson (1993, p. 674) note: 'Learning economics, it seems, may make people more selfish' or 'at least more calculating', seems not to be taken very seriously. By contrast, Frank *et al.* clearly believe that their findings, like previous similar evidence, are *relevant*, and so for at least two reasons.

Firstly, from the purely selfish perspective of economists, it can be argued, as Frank *et al.* do and consistent with the results of several studies, that 'the ultimate victims of noncooperative behavior may be the very people who practice it' (p. 170). And, in fact, as they add, 'the direct pursuit of material self-interest may indeed often be self-defeating'. Thus, paradoxically or perhaps ironically, the rational, self-interested, but hence myopically greedy economists may fare worse and make less money than non-economists in real-life as well as game situations. This was, for instance, the case of the economists, particularly in their role as 'proposers', in the Carter and Irons's (1991) 'Ultimatum Bargaining Game' experiment, as also highlighted by Lattimore (1992).[2] Yet, as Frank (1987, p. 602) points out: 'The clear irony is that the gains from cooperation cannot be fully exploited here [within a honest/dishonest population model] unless one adopts at the outset what everyone would call a genuinely unselfish point of view.'

Secondly, from the broader perspective of society's well-being, it may well be argued that society would benefit from more social cooperation. Indeed, according to Frank *et al.*: 'In an ever more interdependent world, social cooperation has become increasingly important – and yet increasingly fragile' (p. 170). The irony here is, moreover, that, as Stiglitz (1993, pp. 110–11) emphasizes: 'The more ruthlessly individuals pursue their self-interest – the more they behave as we economists teach our students they do behave – the less efficient, in a sense, is the economy.' Therefore, in Frank *et al.*'s concluding words, 'economists may wish to stress a broader view of human motivation in their teaching' (p. 171), than simple self-interest.[3]

S5.1 POSSIBLE EXPLANATIONS FOR ECONOMISTS' OBSERVED 'BAD' BEHAVIOUR

Given the substantial bias in economics toward the neoclassical paradigm – built upon the individualistic, self-interested, rational, utility-maximizing theory of *homo economicus* – it would be surprising, one might argue, if economists (or at least the large majority subscribing to that model) weren't different, and if economics training weren't to influence students' behaviour, besides enhancing their economic understanding. In Frank *et al.*'s words, 'it would be remarkable indeed if none of the observed differences in behavior were the result of repeated and intensive exposure to a model whose unequivocal prediction is that people will defect whenever self-interest dictates' (p. 170).

Nevertheless, as Frank *et al.* rightly stress, before the above conclusions are upheld, alternative explanations of why economists appear to be more selfish and uncooperative need to be considered, in which studying economics may not play any causal role, or may only be partly responsible. In particular, three possible explanations can be envisaged.

Firstly, there may be an element of 'selection bias' to begin with. That is to say, more selfish and greedy individuals, on average more interested in a wealth-maximizing career and for whom maximizing their own income is thus more important than any equity or fairness considerations, may have self-selected into economics. Secondly, there may be a 'sexist bias' amongst economists, since compared to other groups they are usually preponderantly more male. Therefore, since women tend to be more cooperative than men, as Frank *et al.*'s evidence suggests and consistent with other empirical studies also cited in their paper, this can add to the explanation of why economists are observed to be more often *defectors* than are non-economists. Thirdly, there may be a higher expectation amongst economists that any experimental partner is more likely to defect than cooperate. In other words, economists may more often misperceive (and be more inclined to have a 'negative' perception of) partners' behaviour, possibly also as a mirror reflection of their own mainly self-interested motivations. After all, as Frank *et al.* point out, this very expectation is encouraged by the self-interest model – and so its internalization, consciously or subconsciously, should be expected as a natural outcome of 'good' economics training.

However, the results of the Frank *et al.* 'Prisoner's Dilemma' experiment, involving various groups of economics and non-economics students, show that, even after controlling for the influence of gender and the expectations about partner performance, 'defection rates would remain significantly higher for economists than for noneconomists' (p. 167). In addition, the evidence which they present in relation to their 'Honesty Surveys' – conducted by posing a pair of ethical dilemmas to different groups of economics and non-economics students – clearly suggests that, whatever the degree of 'selection bias' may be to start with, studying economics does encourage less cooperative and more cynical (less honest) behaviour, and the more so, the more the emphasis is placed in the economics lectures on the self-interest model.

Yet, it might still be argued that economists' seemingly more selfish and uncooperative behaviour is simply due to there being a compelling pressure among them to perform, in experimental studies, in accordance with the 'categorical' predictions and dictates of the rational self-interest model – thus deliberately disregarding any equity, fairness or distributional considerations, as proof of their very own knowledge and understanding of rational-choice/expected utility theory. But that, in real life, economists' behaviour would not be any different from that of others. (An opposite argument here is that of Yezer, Goldfarb and Poppen (1996), that the more uncooperative performance by economists is simply due to more honesty on their part (see below).)

An alternative suggestion here, reported also by Hausman and McPherson (1993, fn. 4), would be that economists in laboratory experiments behave more selfishly and uncooperatively 'because they grasp the situation better'. Yet, a problem with this interpretation is that the better grasping of the situation by economists – being supposedly more strategically sophisticated and hence more aware of the economic free-riding incentives that imply following the strictly selfish strategy as the only 'rationally' defensible one – seems to result frequently in a worse individual outcome, both in the 'prisoner's dilemma' and the 'ultimatum game'. Thus, if a better knowledge and understanding of both the general economic environment and the specific game being played is supposed and expected to yield a higher individual payoff – that is, if maximizing one's own income is the presumed objective – then it is more often the non-economists, the allegedly less strategically skilled experimental subjects, who by faring better appear to display a clearly superior grasp of the situation.[4]

As to the previous argument which suggests that economists are *not* different in their real life – and which stresses the possible strong pressure on them when participating in lab experiments, to behave in accord with the self-interest model, thus realizing a self-fulfilling expectation on the part of the researchers – the Frank *et al.* results need to be reconsidered accordingly. Clearly, both their 'Prisoner's Dilemma' experiment and 'Honesty Surveys' belong to the 'non-real-life-situation' experiment type. Thus, it might be argued, the results of these tests, while extremely interesting and instructive, may be suffering from this potentially serious drawback and so do not clearly establish that economists behave differently in real life.

By contrast, the Frank *et al.* 'Survey of Charitable Giving' by college professors, carried out via mailed questionnaires, is not a laboratory test and is hence immune from this problem. Assuming truthful reporting by respondents, the survey suggests that economists are more likely than others to free-ride and are 'also among the least generous in terms of their median gifts to large charities', despite their generally higher incomes. However, a criticism could here be raised on the grounds that a refusal to donate to charities may not be free-riding, but may rather be politically/ideologically motivated.[5] That is, what is perceived as more free-riding and easy-riding by economists – less generosity both in their rate of participation and levels of charitable giving – could in principle simply reflect stronger political convictions amongst economists than other academics. (On the other hand, though, the survey indicates that economists were slightly below the sample average in terms of their reported voting frequency in presidential elections. However, using voting behaviour as a test of free-riding could also be clearly criticized, since the reasons why people vote cannot be understood and explained in simple utilitarian terms.[6]) Furthermore, as Frank *et al.* report: 'On a number of other dimensions covered in our survey, the behavior of economists was little different from the behavior of members of other disciplines' (p. 162). Consequently, also this survey's findings, although very suggestive, might still be regarded by some as, all in all, inconclusive.

Moreover, even this type of survey can be criticized on the grounds that what people say (their self-reports in surveys) may not truthfully reflect their actual behaviour, or may in fact badly misrepresent it. Indeed, this particular criticism is raised by Yezer, Goldfarb and Poppen (1996), who offer experimental and survey results contradicting, as they claim, Frank *et al.*'s. They argue that one learns more by watching what people do in real life, than what they say in surveys (for 'talk is cheap'), or how they play in structured laboratory games. For, according to Yezer *et al.*, in surveys or specialized games that are designed to reveal cooperativeness, '(t)here are strong biases toward answering questions in the 'right' way, or in a socially desirable manner . . . Dishonest students may try to conceal noncooperative behavior . . . Students providing the least cooperative responses to the honesty surveys may be the most honest and truthful. Economists might respond more truthfully about a low level of charitable behavior not because they are less generous, but because they are more honest or introspective about behavior' (p. 179). And they go on quoting Hirshleifer's (1994, p. 1) guess 'that economists are not more selfish, but only more acceptant of human behavior'.

Wanting an experiment 'that would reveal the extent of actual cooperation in a real-world setting, not a paper survey or a structured game' (p. 179), Yezer *et al.* thus carried out a 'Lost-Letter' experiment, 'in which envelopes containing currency are dropped in classrooms before classes in economics or other subjects are scheduled to meet. The return rate on lost letters is then used as a measure of cooperation' (p. 180).[7] Contrary to expectations based on Frank *et al.*'s and others' results, their 'experimental evidence indicates that economics students are far more cooperative than students studying other disciplines' (p. 181). Moreover, having also carried out a separate survey of what students expected would happen in such a situation, their 'results suggest that economics students gave answers that were a more truthful reflection of their actual behavior' (p. 184), for the gap between actual return rates and reported return rates was much smaller for them. Finally, they replicated the Frank *et al.* 'Honesty Surveys'. According to their results 'it does not appear that exposure to introductionary economics decreases cooperativeness' (p. 183), or that specific exposure to standard neoclassical economics does even more so. Indeed, their results suggest that classroom teaching does not significantly influence student attitude toward cooperation, while additional evidence they provide suggests that student attitude may be more affected by highly publicized media discussion on, for example, international trade issues.

S5.2 REASONS FOR CONCERN

Having considered all (or at least most of) the possible criticisms to Frank *et al.*'s results and also some contrary evidence, one might conclude that economists are 'normal' after all, and that there is no evident 'negative' economics training effect.

Yet, Frank, Gilovich and Regan (1996), in their reply article to Yezer *et al.*, maintain that the latters' results 'do little to alleviate our original concerns about the effects of economics training' (p. 187). They defend the validity of paper surveys and laboratory experiments. In particular, the latter provide, according to them, a better opportunity to control incentives than natural or field experiments, with the material incentives in laboratory experiments, moreover, closely mimicking the material incentives found in naturally occurring social dilemmas. Indeed, they 'believe that, on balance, the social-dilemma experiments constitute the best available evidence on whether economics training inhibits cooperation' (p. 189), although admitting that '(c)ontext surely matters'. They also acknowledge the ambiguity of the Yezer *et al.* 'Lost-Letter' experiment and classroom surveys, but insist on the general thrust of their own (1993) and others' findings that economics students are less cooperative than others and that they become even less so as they go on studying economics – all this hence providing considerable evidence in favour of a training effect.

Moreover, as they point out, there is evidence that expectations even only slightly biased in favour of cooperation tend to be self-fulfilling, and that, when facing social dilemmas and often having the option of simply not playing, 'people who elect to play are disproportionately those who expect their partners to cooperate, and who, in turn, are much more likely to cooperate themselves' (p. 191). It then follows that '(b)y emphasizing the prevalence of opportunism, economics training may lead students not to engage, thereby relegating the fruits of cooperation to more optimistic members of the population. It is thus by no means clear that economists do their students a favor by inculcating cynicism about the altruism of others. In fact, students who end up basing their expectations on a literal interpretation of the self-interest model are almost certainly harmed' (p. 191).

Thus, as they conclude 'three important points remain clear. First, . . . economics training encourages the view that people are motivated primarily by self-interest. Second, there is clear evidence that this view leads to expect others to defect in social dilemmas . . . Third, there is also clear evidence that when people expect their partners to defect in social dilemmas, they are overwhelmingly likely to defect themselves' (p. 192).

All this may clearly not appeal to mainstream economists, who might still not want to admit or recognize that their own behaviour may be different and that studying economics, as generally taught at present, may well be a 'corrupting force': it may have a 'negative' influence on students' values and behaviour, fostering and enhancing self-interest and inhibiting cooperation. And as Etzioni (1988) argues, 'if it is true that people do seek to balance their pleasures with moral considerations, and if they are taught, to the contrary, that they are 'really' only out to maximize their pleasure (and all that follows, that people behave morally only as long as it pays, and so on), there is likely to be a negative, anti-moral effect' (p. 251).

Yet, the existence of a generally broad agreement even amongst economists on the beneficial effects that a more altruistic and cooperative behaviour would have on the society as a whole, as well as on the very individuals who practise it, combined with the clearly disturbing evidence by Frank *et al.* and others, *should* encourage some 'positive' changes in economics teaching, and introductory (micro)economics in particular. And that evidence should also encourage and enhance economic research analysis based both on a wider understanding of individual preferences, motivations and behavioural rules, and on the possibility of their endogeneity to the system.

6 Ethics, Game Theory and Laboratory Experiments

INTRODUCTION

Both political and economic analyses and activities, it has been argued, can and should be subject to moral appraisal, and indeed judged in moral terms and with the same moral criteria. Here, a similar claim is made for game-theoretic and laboratory experimental analyses and applications concerning individuals' behaviour in general, and economic behaviour in particular. The concern here is not so much with the possible relevance of game theory and experimental economics to moral philosophy – whether in their normative or positive applications which attempt to determine, predict or analyse 'moral' conduct or 'moral' solutions to problems of strategic interactions among individuals. Rather the concern here is with some of the moral presuppositions and potential ethical implications of both game theory and laboratory tests.

6.1 FROM GAME PLAYING TO GAME THEORY

Playing games is what we learn to do as children. We learn the rules of games, and the aim of games: to win. We also learn the difference between two kinds of game. The first is *patience-solitaire*, where the 'entertainment' aspect – pastime – plays a crucial role, alongside the aim and desire to win. The second is a *group game* (for example, board game or parlour game), played with one or more other players. Here, there is the 'socialization' aspect – interacting with others – as well as the aim and desire to win. Some players have a more developed 'competitive' attitude than others: their desire or struggle to win is stronger and, if they lose, they therefore become much more upset than others. Some have, by contrast, a more developed 'participative' attitude: to them playing with others is relatively more important than actually being the winner. Thus, the competitive/aggressive player may win more often, pointing to an element of self-fulfilling expectation, as a result of the different attitude and behaviour. A third aspect, in this second type of game, is the 'team' attitude, for the game in which pairing or teaming up is required. Here there is no logical presumption on whether the competitive rather than the participative player is better at it, for a highly competitive player may well obstruct or interfere with the team play.

6.1.1 From Playing Games to Working...

Having learned how to play games, we then go to school and learn how to work, where the rules are different requiring in particular: discipline, effort, meeting deadlines, . . . Here, our acquired abilities in playing games may not help (that is, may not be transferable) and often are, in fact, irrelevant: a good athlete is, for instance, not necessarily a good reader or writer. Clearly, some skills we have developed in playing games may help. In general, however, the context/situation is now completely different, and different rules apply and need to be learned. Whether a good and successful *game player* is also a good and successful *worker* (*student*) is, therefore, not in any way easily predictable, as the two activities usually involve very different characteristics.

Thus, learning how to distinguish between different contexts/situations is part of the learning process, of human development or 'maturation'. Indeed, those who do not learn this basic and crucial point are normally regarded as immature and childish.

6.1.2 ... to Game Theory

Yet game theorists, who apply game-theoretic analyses and methods to all sorts of possible situations, appear generally to overlook this essential point. Thus, they assume, for example, the same game structure, rules and aims in the case of all potential 'Prisoner's Dilemma' (PD) settings, independently of the 'what, where and when' questions.

The existence of a specific 'conflict of interests' between the players – where the players' interests are *not* completely (but only partly) opposed and their payoffs (utilities) are accordingly ranked in a particular way – is used as the rationale/justification for applying the same PD game structure, rules and aims. But this is a very weak motivation, given the importance of the 'nature' of the conflict. For not only may the PD game be a *safe* or a *risky* one (depending on the specific payoff parameter values); or else a *negative* or a *positive* one (depending on whether the game involves minimizing losses (for example, years in jail), or maximizing gains (for example, money prizes)); and this may well imply non-symmetry in players' behaviour. But the PD game may also involve a *double conflict* – as in the classic case of the two prisoners, or in the case of duopolistic firms, with one conflict being between the two players, and the other being between the two players on the one hand, and society on the other.[1] Or it may involve only *one conflict*, that between the two players – as in the case of an imaginary 'gambling casino that offers a PD table', assuming here that the casino's own interest (minimizing its cash prizes to its two customers/players) is of no 'real' concern to society.[2] And, indeed, the PD game may have *moral content and implications* (as in the case of the prisoners, or duopoly), or may be just a 'friendly' game with no moral content or implications (as in the case of the gambling casino offering a PD table).

Thus the two players' cooperative or non-cooperative behaviour may well be differently judged by an observer/spectator (whether impartial or interested) or by society, according indeed to whether it is a PD game with or without moral connotations. Hence, depending on the PD type or context, 'cheating' (that is, defecting) might not carry the same (negative) weight or moral condemnation. Likewise, 'cooperation' can have different – positive or negative – meanings and so involve a different moral valuation. For it may refer to beneficial cooperative behaviour, as in the case of an individual's voluntary contribution to public goods; or it may signify 'conspiracy' or 'collusion', as in the case of the two prisoners or duopolistic firms.[3] (Similarly, 'loyalty' may have a positive or negative meaning, depending on whether it is, for example, to one's family, friends or employer, or else to a criminal organization, as in the case of mafia loyalty, *omertà*. And even 'altruism' may have positive or negative connotations, depending on whether it is accompanied by reason (that is, 'rational altruism') and is 'pure', or else is merely an instinctive/emotional force (for example, the mother's love for a son, in which case it may well be 'blind') and/or is not pure (that is, 'enlightened self-interest' or 'reciprocal altruism'.)

This clearly emphasizes the constant need for individuals' discriminating judgement; in other words, to learn, use or devise simple behavioural rules is *not* sufficient to ensure appropriate or moral behaviour in all situations. This further emphasizes how game theory may well be misleading in its predictions, or devoid of any significant content – for in analysing and drawing the same conclusions for situations which, albeit theoretically similar in their strategic structure, may *de facto* be extremely diverse or even opposite, it does not take into account individuals' critical judgement of the specific context.[4]

Moreover and relatedly, the use of the same game structure, rules and aims for all possible PDs is also symptomatic/indicative of the total dismissal of the relevance of human learning and experience, of cultures, values, ethical and social norms, in determining the actual solution to a conflict, and hence in sensibly predicting its resolution. For the same conflict may well be, and often is, solved in different ways, depending on the specific environment in which it arises – as, for instance, in the case of worker–employer conflict solutions in, for example, Germany, Italy or Great Britain.

Thus, game theory often fails to predict how 'players' actually play. If this were all there was to it, one could (in principle) simply dismiss or ignore game theory, letting game theorists play their own game, without paying (much) attention to them. However, and unfortunately, there is much more to it. For not only has game theory become a 'core' part of many academic disciplines – notably economics, sociology, psychology, law, politics, biology – and hence many and ever-increasing numbers of students learn about it, and may well then be influenced by its 'logic'; but it has also become a 'tool' (likewise Cost/Benefit analysis) regularly used by a variety and growing number of decision-makers – policy-makers, business managers, military strategists, and so on.

It can be argued that the 'dangers' of game theory are similar and, in fact, linked to those of neoclassical economics and are very real: individuals are affected by it and decisions are made in its name. A moral reappraisal of game theory is, therefore, not only important but indeed necessary and a duty for any ethical person.

6.2. CONCERN FOR OTHERS IN GAMES VERSUS REAL-LIFE

If I *play poker* (or some other card game), or if I *play monopoly* (or some other board game), my degree of altruism, if any, does not generally affect or interfere with my playing. If I am playing a competitive (zero-sum) game, and if I am a truly 'sportive' player – that is, aiming to win – I will have *no concern* whatsoever for other players (family members, friends or others). My only real concern will be to win. Although, apart from my personal playing skills or abilities and beside my game luck, the extent of my desire to win – that is, my commitment to or involvement in the game – may well affect how well I play. In other words, my 'attitude' to game-playing is likely to be very crucial in determining my winning chances.

Somewhat similar may be my approach to 'playing', if I am part of a *laboratory experiment* – no matter how well thought-out the experimental design is. That is, regardless of how close the laboratory experiment may be to a real-life situation, I am obviously aware of the fact that I am participating in such a test, with no real-life consequences for anybody else taking part similarly in the experiment. The only 'real' effect may be how my playing can affect the final 'monetary' payoffs to myself and possibly to others, within the range of payments determined for that particular experiment, if any. I may, undoubtedly, take the experiment very seriously and try to play as well and/or as 'rationally' as possible, perhaps also in consideration of how my playing might be judged by the 'professionals' conducting the experiment (who may indeed be my own teachers). However, my potential feelings, if any, for any other participating player(s) are likely to be well checked by my clear knowledge of being 'simply' part of an experiment or game. Once more, though, my 'attitude' to game-playing may be a significant determinant for the outcome of the game. Am I a truly 'competitive' player, or am I a not very committed one who believes that what is more important in a game is taking part and the fun involved rather than the final score? Certainly, the experiment may be a non-zero-sum game, so that 'winning' may well require cooperative play rather than competitive play. But the point remains that it still is a 'game', and not an actual occurrence in my daily life, even if the game/experiment may describe a situation extremely similar to situations encountered in my real life.

Finally, if I am a *child*, I may have a tendency to approach even 'real life' non-game situations as if they were games. Therefore, I may be acting as a player in a game, even if the situation is in fact not a game at all. And, no doubt, this may also be the case for many immature and indeed 'childish' adults, who seem to go through life thinking that it is all a game.

Setting aside all the above situations – that is, playing cards or board games, or participating in a laboratory experiment, or being a child or a childish adult – *real life* presents every individual with situations in which choices and decisions have to be made, and/or a behaviour has to be chosen, which will also normally affect other individuals and not simply on purely materialistic grounds. Our own 'concern' and/or even prior realization of how our choices, decisions or behaviour will or might affect others is likely to have a major impact on our very choices, decisions or behaviour.

Concern for others may be based on love, or altruism, fairness, justice, . . . And the extent of concern can clearly vary between absolute lack of concern to extreme concern – even possibly excessive concern, to the point of consequent potential inaction or inability to take decisions, or else of consequent undesirable or damaging (albeit unintended) effects on others. Also, total lack of concern for others may be due to individual narrow *selfishness* (nasty case), or to genuine, perhaps naive, *unawareness* of the effects of our choices and actions on other individuals (non-nasty case).

Altruism – love or concern for others and for their 'general' well-being, and so not only in terms of their materialistic welfare – is obviously a crucial factor in determining an individual's course of action or behaviour. Thus, for example, in deciding between two jobs in two different locations, I may or may not also take into account how my choice will possibly affect my spouse's and/or children's social and working life, friendship, schools, . . . – beside deciding on the basis of my 'preference' for one job or the other in the 'normal' economic terms of career prospect, work environment, salary and monetary rewards in general, including, that is, all the potential pecuniary 'perks'. But apart from altruism, *sense of honesty, fairness, justice, commitment, duty,* . . . can also play a crucial role in shaping an individual's choices, decisions or behaviour.

Altruism, honesty, fairness, sense of justice, as well as commitment or duty, may naturally have a different meaning or significance in the context of a game (if and when applicable), as compared to a real-life context. Thus, for example, cheating at poker (or at cards, or at play in general) is clearly a dishonest action – a 'good' poker player will no doubt bluff, but not cheat.[5] However, the implication of the dishonest player's cheating, no matter how despicable, is of a different 'nature' from that of, for instance, a dishonest worker/employee. In the case of poker, honest players may, of course, lose money as a result of someone else cheating; but they have, after all, entered the game knowing that losing money was a possibility, independently of whether or not other players would cheat.[6] Conversely, in the case of a dishonest worker – one who, for example, slacks when unsupervised (lacking any sense of duty), or who steals from the workplace – the consequences of his dishonesty on the employer and/or other employees may well be economically or financially very serious in the medium or long term, as well as the action also being (morally) unacceptable and indeed legally punishable (unlike, usually, dishonest poker playing).[7]

Likewise, lack of love or altruism or compassion for a fellow game player cannot generally be (morally) compared with a similar lack of concern for, e.g. a family member or neighbour or colleague, or even possibly a stranger, in a non-game but real-life situation. Uncaring game-playing can certainly 'hurt' other players, as well as make them lose. But it cannot ever carry the same (moral) implications as does the uncaring for others, and especially 'close' individuals in real life. For *a game is a game, while life is not a game.*

6.3 LABORATORY EXPERIMENTS AND 'MIXED' RESULTS

Laboratory experiments producing 'mixed' results are not normally welcomed by the economic researchers conducting the experiment, since 'mixed' results imply somewhat inconclusive findings. Thus, whatever hypotheses were tested, it is not possible to assert with any certainty that those hypotheses have been either supported or rejected by the evidence. However, the very search for some conclusive answers, about the behaviour of individuals or of economic agents in particular, is somewhat misplaced or at best naive, revealing the researchers' very belief in, and/or need of, some ultimate and unconfutable truth about human nature and conduct. This is clearly symptomatic, as well as the consequence, of the claim and belief that economics is a positive, objective, scientific discipline – indeed a 'science'. In fact, the search and struggle for economic truths and foundations reflect a particular, although often undeclared or unconscious, philosophical stand on the part of the theoretician, and even more so, arguably, of the applied researcher.

On the one hand, orthodox economists genuinely believe in the undisputable multiplicity of individuals' subjective preferences. No economist would, of course, ever claim that one should expect a particular bundle of preferences to prevail. It is simply accepted that individuals' tastes and preferences differ, as a matter of fact. Economists can possibly argue about whether tastes are exogenously given or fixed, as innate factors, or whether they are, at least to some extent, endogenously determined, and whether they may change and if so how.[8] And economists can also argue about both the role and relevance of (given) constraints in affecting individual choices, and whether constraints may, at times at least and to some extent, be also endogenously determined.

On the other hand, however, mainstream economists expect and presuppose a uniform (homogeneous and invariant) behaviour by individuals as economic agents. That is, human beings are all supposed

goodness being indeed judged by the effects or consequences they have, since it is only the effects or results of those acts which have an intrinsic value, independently of the intention or moral motivation of the actions; such a 'teleological' view, coupled with the conviction that there are (if only to be discovered) clear and sure philosophical universal 'foundations' for knowledge and action based on rational principles, is generally embraced (albeit often unconsciously) by economists – as is the idea of, and hence search for, the 'truth' and some universal principles.[11]

The extreme belief by economists in 'rationality', and in particular in the economic (instrumental) conception of rationality – thus rejecting other, equally legitimate and possibly ethically superior, concepts of rationality – appears to be above all the result of the economists' attempts at, and pretence of, establishing economics as a 'science', similar to a natural science. Consequently, economic reasoning, explanations and predictions have to be founded on rational, internally logical and coherent sets of principles. But, the excessive belief in, and exaltation of, rationality and reason (the credo of rationalism), together with the refusal to accept the near impossibility of actually establishing economic principles in a proper 'scientific' manner (as for the case of moral principles), have somehow turned economists into dogmatists. Their 'faith' in economic rationality is not only in plain contradiction with the alleged scientific/positivistic nature of economics, but is also clearly counterproductive, in so far as attempts are made at explaining and predicting economic agents' behaviour. For such misplaced belief, turned into faith, can actually prevent economists from gaining any reasonable understanding of how economic decisions are made and of how they may subsequently be modified.[12]

A further implication is the economists' prompt, albeit generally non-motivated, reliance on psychological/emotive theories of human nature and behaviour – where instincts, impulses, passions (to regret or rejoice) make an entry – in order to account for some conducts, otherwise unexplained and unexplainable by orthodox economic theory. And along a similar and related line, the ready acceptance of biological, evolutionary and/or genetical theories of human nature and behaviour. The endorsement of psychological as well as biological (evolutionary/genetical) factors and theories seems, in fact, to sit more comfortably with the neoclassical economists' 'act of faith' in the free-standing individuals' own self-determination.

Indeed, the relevance and significance of 'individualism' for economists is so axiomatically and dogmatically overriding that any philosophical position or theory, stressing the importance of the 'moral dimension' in understanding human choices and behaviour, is not only ignored but actively opposed – as also remarked by Etzioni (1988, p. 12). For it would amount, in part at least, to embracing a 'deontological' position with regard to human acts – a position centred on the principle of duty (*deon*) or obligation, which stresses that the moral goodness of an act should be judged by its intention or motivation, and not by its consequences, and which therefore attributes intrinsic value to features of the act itself. But this obviously conflicts with the mainstream utilitarian, consequentialist or teleological, neoclassical position. And it would, moreover, imply rather devastating consequences for economic analysis. Indeed, as Broome (1992, p. 282) points out, in his discussion of Etzioni's (1988) book, *The Moral Dimension*, 'If deontological moralities affect people's behavior in important ways, then economics is in for a shock.'[13]

7 Competitive vs Cooperative Individuals and Moral Principles of Cooperation

INTRODUCTION

Cooperation among individuals both in everyday life and laboratory tests is a common phenomenon. Indeed significant cooperation occurs even in a most hostile environment, such as that of the one-shot Prisoner's Dilemma, for which game theory and economics predict, as for other less troublesome situations, the 'rational' but inefficient non-cooperative outcome.

The question thus arises of how cooperation can be accounted for. One answer is provided by game theorists themselves. Their attempts to explain or justify cooperation conceive of rational players cooperating for their own personal advantage. Endorsing a teleological (consequentialist) moral theory, cooperation is accordingly seen, within both the neoclassical utilitarian and contractarian traditions, as the result of an individualistic calculus, that is, as instrumental in furthering one's own interest. Considering this position is the first objective here.

An alternative approach, however, is to take a deontological position with respect to human acts in general and cooperative behaviour in particular. Cooperation can thus be seen as driven by morality, which entails self-imposed restraints on personal choices, and may even turn constraints into preferences.[1] Following this latter approach, the second (main) aim here is to consider moral principles and rules which prescribe cooperation as the standard of conduct. The analysis identifies six specific cases leading to *natural* or *command* cooperative behaviour (in a sense to be later clarified).

The outline of this chapter is as follows. Section 7.1 briefly reviews the issues of (economic) 'rationality' and 'rational play' as posited by standard game theory, stressing both the apparent weakness of the theory's predictive and explanatory powers and its endeavour at rationalizing cooperative play. Section 7.2 provides a quick review of the Prisoner's Dilemma and three other, also known, Social Dilemmas (all described in Appendix 7.1), focusing on the characteristics of the four types of 'competitive' players, both in terms of their specific preferences and their resulting strategies. (A brief analysis of the six asymmetric games obtained by crossing the four 'competitive' players' preferences is in Appendix 7.2.) This provides the analytical, game-theoretic, background (no doubt redundant for those familiar with Social Dilemmas) for discussing, in the next section, the essential features of six types of 'cooperative' individuals. Section 7.3 thus offers a somewhat novel analysis of moral ('ethical' or 'biblical') cooperators and of their characteristics and relative cooperative strength. Clearly, all 'cooperative' individuals do not truly face a Social Dilemma. But what motivates their cooperative conduct differs from case to case. Therefore the analysis considers how well different underlying moral principles can sustain social, economic and moral cooperation. And it suggests that individual private (secular) morality is, in this aim, perhaps superior to religion, although undoubtedly more demanding on the individual. A brief summary is given in Section 7.4.

7.1 GAME THEORY, RATIONALITY AND COOPERATION

Most game theory purports to predict or prescribe human behaviour in situations of conflict of interest among individuals. Yet, its predictions are not very good and often unsatisfactory, plainly contradicting individuals' actual behaviour, as empirically observed in real-life circumstances or experimental conditions, especially in relation to cooperation.[2]

Game theorists' prescriptions are typically based on the assumption that 'rational' play is narrowly self-interested play. In this conventional sense, individual 'rationality' simply means that individuals select their own options or strategy so as to maximize their (expected) utility, defined in terms of (subjective) preferences. 'Rational choice' is hence instrumental to individual utility maximization or preference satisfaction: rationality implies choosing efficient means for the attainment of given ends.

These prescriptions can certainly be the wrong ones for a 'rational' player to act on if the other player is 'irrational'. But the recommendations may also be wrong if it were not to be rational to play in a purely self-interested manner. This possibility clearly depends on the game being played. Indeed, even if, regardless of the game, the aim and desire of all 'rational' players is to win, winning need not require playing on the dictate of pure self-interest. For example, in the case of 'total war' *zero-sum* games – where one player's gain is another's loss – 'rational' players should naturally follow the theory's prescriptions.

Two perfectly rational players playing against each other ought (and are expected) to independently further their conflicting, and indeed completely opposed, interests. However, the situation may be different in the case of *non-zero-sum* games – where players' interests are not totally opposed – and in particular when by their joint action players can increase the common good or collective outcome, as for instance in a 'coordination' game. Here, players who were to act on the standard 'rational' play dictate, and hence only pursue their own separate objectives, could reasonably be said not to be playing rationally. For, if cooperation is in both players' own best and mutual interest, choosing the prescribed non-cooperative option undermines the common good and prevents achieving the best outcome possible.

Therefore, the 'rational' pursuit of self-interest may not be rational, after all, and may well be self-defeating. For, to reiterate, in terms of game theory and its underpinning 'rational choice' theory, 'rational' choices are those leading to the maximization of a player's utility, and this is clearly not the case when a supposedly 'rational' player ends up worse off than he would have done, had he followed a different – allegedly 'less rational' or 'irrational' – course of action.

Two main explanations for this evident shortcoming of the theory have been put forward by a number of authors.[3] Firstly, game theory prescribes that, in making their choices, rational players should treat the actions of their opponents as if they were 'states of nature', that is, exogenous events. But this may be an inappropriate, or even incoherent, recommendation for rational individuals who are playing games against other similarly rational individuals – rather than games against nature – since opponents' choices represent, in a sense, an endogenous type of uncertainty. That is to say, the idea that players' strategies are chosen 'independently' seems questionable when each player's choice of strategy depends on his 'subjective' (probability) assessment over the strategy choices of other rational players, and not on 'subjective' beliefs about states of nature.[4] Secondly, the theory's prescriptions are always addressed to game players as independent individuals. But in many problems of strategic interaction such as 'coordination' games players should rather be seen as members of the same team in a game against nature, or against another team. And recommendations should thus be addressed to them as team-players rather than as independent players. For, here, the proper and 'rational' perspective for players to adopt is not an individualistic one but a collective one.[5]

What is indeed under criticism is a crucial assumption of game theory, that of *common knowledge of rationality* (CKR).[6] For CKR may not be sufficient to lead rational players to Nash equilibria, and, besides, not all Nash equilibria are rational solutions. And CKR may even be incoherent (and hence should not be assumed) in certain games, where there seems to be an element of circularity in the players' decision-making process.[7] Some alternative assumptions have thus been suggested, such as that of *entrenched common belief in rationality*, which though embodies the same (expected utility theory) concept of rationality as does CKR.[8] More fundamentally, arguing that it is the standard conception of economic rationality that is unsatisfactory, other views of rationality have been proposed, such as that of *resolute* choice, which may be especially useful in overcoming conflicts between individual rationality and social optimality.[9]

Acknowledging that cooperation is a widespread phenomenon, many game theorists, economists and moral philosophers, rather than asking how 'rational' players ought to act, ask how cooperation can rationally be justified. Attempts to justify cooperation centre mainly on the Prisoner's Dilemma, but similarly apply to other less difficult Social Dilemmas, and take several forms.

To start with, a crucial distinction is made between a one-shot Prisoner's Dilemma game and a repeated game, and then between a finitely-repeated and an infinitely-repeated game. Thus, in the former case of a one-time-only game, non-cooperation, it is claimed, is bound to arise as the only 'rational' strategy, since players are compelled by logic to defect. Likewise, in a finitely-iterated game, defection on every round is also claimed to be the 'rational' choice, as the 'backward-induction' argument proves, although leading (admittedly) to paradoxical implications. However, it is normally accepted that cooperation can be 'rational', in the case of an infinitely-repeated game.

In this latter case, cooperation can be justified on the basis of (self-interested) 'reputation building' considerations. Moreover, even in a finitely-repeated game, reputation building can lead to cooperative behaviour. In particular, if players have incomplete information about their opponents' 'type' (that is, whether competitive or cooperative types), then to build a reputation for being cooperative or altruistic – by, for example, playing a 'tit-for-tat' strategy – can be in one's best interest.[10] Thus, according to this 'rationality' hypothesis, there is no need for 'irrational' or 'altruistic' types to actually exist, but only that there are sufficient beliefs among players that such types exist.[11] Conversely, according to the 'warm-glow' hypothesis of altruism – where individuals are assumed to care about the act of being nice to each other, and so attach some private value to the act of giving, deriving pleasure or 'moral satisfaction' from, for example, contributing to the public good –[12] some individuals actually are of the 'altruistic' or 'cooperative' type.

As well as egoistic or self-regarding incentives like reputation (or 'image') or reciprocity (or 'reciprocal altruism'), other 'sentiments' or 'emotions' are also appealed to in order to justify cooperative behaviour on the part of self-interested 'rational' players, such as the need for social approval, or the possibility of reliably signalling an honest conscience as a sort of commitment device.[13] And cooperation can also obtain by incorporating into game theory and economics other 'emotions' such as 'fairness' considerations, where players' payoffs do not simply depend on their actions, but also on their *beliefs* about other players' motives or intentions – pointing to a sort of 'reciprocal fairness' or 'contingent altruism'.[14]

Cooperation can also be 'rational' for selfish rational players, if communication is possible and pre-commitment devices are available, and if legally-binding enforceable agreements can be reached. In particular, in a repeated game, cooperation can rationally be sustained by credible threats of punishment, that is, when the punishment strategy or the implicit or explicit threat of retaliation is not an empty one. More generally, mutual restraints on individual non-cooperative behaviour can be enforced by coercive rules and sanctions, and cooperation can be stimulated through collectively imposed inducements or incentives to individuals' own private interests. Moreover, some Prisoner's Dilemma games can be said to be 'safe' – in view of the actual payoff values – and hence 'rational' players can be expected to cooperate since the risk of cooperating is relatively small, compared to that of 'risky' games where much more is at stake.[15]

In addition, evolutionary (sociobiological) arguments have been made that natural (or cultural) selection can sustain cooperative behaviour even in a one-shot Prisoner's Dilemma. Accordingly, some individuals inherit a genetic (or cultural) tendency to cooperate, and the more likely it is that such individuals interact among themselves, the more likely it is that cooperation will prevail. Though here individuals do not consciously choose their strategies; rather their actions are programmed by their genetic structure, or else determined by copying or imitating the behaviour of parents, neighbours, or successful role models.[16]

Finally, and excluding the case of players' irrationality, errors or confusion, it is generally conceded that cooperation can obtain even in a one-shot game, and can be maintained in repeated single-shot games (where there is clearly no possibility of reputation building, or of punishment), if players have genuine or pure 'altruistic preferences' or objectives, or if they behave *as if* they were altruistic, or else if they *are* altruistic and/or cooperative. This is precisely the perspective which will be taken in Section 7.3.

7.2 COMPETITIVE INDIVIDUALS: PRISONER'S DILEMMA AND OTHER SOCIAL DILEMMAS

Among all relevant problems of strategic interaction between individuals, the most famous and most analysed game is the Prisoner's Dilemma. But there are also, as is well known, other situations of conflict of interest.[17]

In particular, considering only two-person, two-strategy *symmetric* games, where both players share the same preferences and hence receive the same payoffs under similar circumstances, there are altogether four familiar *social dilemmas*: the Prisoner's Dilemma, Deadlock, Chicken and Stag Hunt. (See Appendix 7.1 for their description.) They can all be encountered in real-life social and economic interactions, and they all represent *true* dilemmas – in the sense that there is a temptation to defect rather than cooperate with the other player. (Indeed, in the case of Deadlock, both players actually prefer mutual defection to mutual cooperation, so that this is not a very troublesome dilemma, if one at all.[18])

Each player's two strategies are either to cooperate (C) or defect (D). A player who cooperates can get a *reward* payoff if the opponent also cooperates (CC), or else a *sucker* payoff if the other defects (CD). Conversely, a player who defects can get a *punishment* payoff if the opponent also defects (DD), or else a *temptation* (or *free-rider*'s) payoff if the opponent cooperates (DC).

The way in which the payoffs are ordered in terms of preferences, that is, the players' payoff ranking, is the distinguishing feature among the four 'social dilemmas'. In all four games, a player always prefers mutual cooperation (CC) over being the lone cooperator (a sucker: CD), that is, CC > CD; also, a player always prefers being the lone defector (DC) over mutual defection (DD), that is, DC > DD. In addition, for the games to be 'true' dilemmas – where a temptation to defect exists – there must be an element of *greed* (an incentive to defect when the other cooperates), and/or of *mistrust* – *fear* of ending up as a sucker (hence an incentive to defect when the other defects). That is, DC > CC due to *greed* and/or DD > CD due to *fear*.[19] Both *greed* and *fear* are present in the Prisoner's Dilemma and in Deadlock. By contrast, in

Chicken there is only the element of *greed*, and in Stag Hunt only *fear*.[20]

A summary of 'competitive' players' social dilemmas is presented in Table 7.1. The top part of the Table depicts a game's 'payoff-matrix' – a table that shows the strategies and related payoffs for the two players, with the first entry in each cell giving the 'row' player's payoff and the second the 'column' player's. And it also lists the conditions needed for a true dilemma to exist.

The centre part of the Table reviews the four 'social dilemmas'. The numbers in each cell represent the utilities, or points, attached by a player to each of the four possible outcomes, where the best outcome scores 3, the second best 2, the next to the last 1, and the worst outcome 0. The numbers in boldface represent a *Nash equilibrium* solution – a pair of strategies such that each is best given the other, that is, when each player chooses the best strategy, given the strategy being chosen by the other.[21] When, moreover, a player has a best strategy no matter what the other does, that is, regardless of the strategy chosen by the other, then that is a *dominant strategy*. And when both players have a dominant strategy, the outcome is a *dominant equilibrium* solution.

Both the Prisoner's Dilemma and Deadlock have a unique Nash dominant equilibrium solution – the non-cooperative outcome, where both players' dominant strategy is to defect. However, in the case of the Prisoner's Dilemma, such a solution is suboptimal (as both players would be better off under mutual cooperation); whereas it is the all-round best solution in the Deadlock game (for mutual cooperation represents only a second-best collective outcome, and so both players should defect as neither of them really wants to cooperate).

In contrast, Chicken and Stag Hunt have no dominant equilibrium solution, but both have two Nash equilibria. In Chicken, both players want to do the opposite of whatever the other does, and the game's two Nash equilibria are where one player cooperates and the other defects. In Stag Hunt, both players prefer to do the same as the other (a 'matching' strategy), and moreover both prefer mutual cooperation to mutual defection, so they should both cooperate; indeed mutual cooperation is a Nash equilibrium. A dilemma should not exist: it is only the *fear* that the other may defect that provides an incentive to defect. Mutual defection is thus a second Nash equilibrium, but Pareto-inferior to the cooperative outcome. This is why Stag Hunt is also called 'trust dilemma' or 'assurance game' or 'coordination game': if only players could trust each other and feel assured of the other's cooperation, then they would no doubt cooperate.

Table 7.1 'Competitive' Individuals: (Two-player, Two-strategy) Social Dilemmas

Payoff-Matrix for two Players, A and B

Payoff Legenda

Reward for mutual cooperation (CC)
Punishment for mutual defection (DD)
Temptation for lone defection (DC)
Sucker for lone cooperation (CD)

		B: C	B: D
A	C	CC, CC	CD, DC
	D	DC, CD	DD, DD

Conditions for a 'True' Dilemma to exist

(i) CC > CD (iii) DC > CC 'Greed' } Incentives
(ii) DC > DD and/or (iv) DD > CD 'Fear' } to Defect

Symmetric games: Four 'Social Dilemmas'

1. **Prisoner's Dilemma (PD)**
   Greed and Fear DC > CC > DD > CD

   1 Nash dominant equilibrium
   (suboptimal non-cooperative outcome)

A \ B	C	D
C	2, 2	0, 3
D	3, 0	**1, 1**

2. **Deadlock (DL)**
   Greed and Fear DC > DD > CC > CD

   1 Nash dominant equilibrium
   (optimal non-cooperative outcome)

A \ B	C	D
C	1, 1	0, 3
D	3, 0	**2, 2**

3. **Chicken (CH)**
   Greed DC > CC > CD > DD

   2 'pure strategy' Nash equilibria
   + 1 'mixed strategy' Nash equilibrium

A \ B	C	D
C	2, 2	**1, 3**
D	**3, 1**	0, 0

4. **Stag Hunt (SH)**
   Fear CC > DC > DD > CD

   2 Nash equilibria
   (optimal cooperative outcome & suboptimal non-coop.)

A \ B	C	D
C	**3, 3**	0, 2
D	2, 0	**1, 1**

Asymmetric games: Six 'Human Conflict' Cross-Models

1\. **PD** / **DL**

PD \ DL	C	D
C	2, 1	0, 3
D	3, 0	**1, 2**

1 Nash dominant equil.

2\. **PD** / **CH**

PD \ CH	C	D
C	2, 2	0, 3
D	**3, 1**	1, 0

1 Nash equilibrium

3\. **PD** / **SH**

PD \ SH	C	D
C	2, 3	0, 2
D	3, 0	**1, 1**

1 Nash equil.(suboptimal)

4\. **(Bully)** **CH** / **DL**

CH \ DL	C	D
C	2, 1	**1, 3**
D	3, 0	0, 2

1 Nash equilibrium

5\. **CH** / **SH**

CH \ SH	C	D
C	2, 3	1, 2
D	3, 0	0, 1

No pure-strategy Nash equil.

6\. **DL** / **SH**

DL \ SH	C	D
C	1, 3	0, 2
D	3, 0	**2, 1**

1 Nash equilibrium

The bottom part of Table 7.1 introduces *asymmetric* games, where the two players do not share the same preferences. By crossing the preferences of the four social dilemmas players, it is possible to derive six hybrid models of conflicts of interest. Among these, the game of Bully – a cross between Chicken and Deadlock – is perhaps the best known (see Appendix 7.1 for its description). (A brief analysis of these cross-models can be found in Appendix 7.2.)

To conclude this section, the four 'competitive' players' strategies are here summarized. No matter with whom they play, both the Prisoner's Dilemma and Deadlock players always defect. When playing against either of the latter, a Chicken player always cooperates (gives in), whilst a Stag Hunt player always defects. When playing against each other, the Chicken and Stag Hunt players do not know what to do with certainty, and hence use some random device or, somewhat equivalently, make their choices based on 'subjective beliefs' or 'conjectures' about the other's choice.

7.3 COOPERATIVE INDIVIDUALS: *NATURAL* OR *COMMAND* COOPERATORS

The objective here is to envisage moral rules of behaviour that prescribe cooperation as the norm.[22] Altogether, six cases are identified and discussed.[23]

Moving from 'competitive' to 'cooperative' games, one should modify the terminology attached to individuals' pairwise preferences over payoffs.[24] Also, now, instead of there being just two individuals, one may more properly think of one individual on one side, and the rest of society on the other. The payoff notation (DC, CC, DD, CD) – where the first letter indicates an individual's own choice of behaviour, and the second letter the behaviour by the rest of society – thus stresses the fact that an individual can choose to be a non-cooperator (defector) or a cooperator in a cooperative society (DC or CC), and similarly to be a non-cooperator or a cooperator in a non-cooperative society (DD or CD).

Kolm (1983), in his outstanding essay 'Altruism and Efficiency', takes the different view (and hence notation) of an individual choosing to be an egoist (e) or an altruist (a), in either an egoistic (E) or altruistic (A) society.[25] Kolm's analysis is totally endorsed here, and indeed according to the view of morality as *altruism cum rationality* (or 'rational altruism'), which has been given in previous chapters, one can say that the 'true' moral choice for an individual is whether to be an egoist or an altruist. However, in the present context, the focus is on alternative ethical theories and moral principles and rules which do all prescribe cooperation, and yet may not all necessarily regard cooperation as an outcome of altruism. This is, notably, the case of 'Kantian' rationality and morality, where cooperation is prescribed, according to the 'categorical imperative', by a universalizable principle based upon reason, and not upon love or altruism. Also, the principle of 'cooperative utilitarianism' may be said ultimately to rest upon an (enlightened self-interested) 'ethical calculus', rather than upon genuine altruism.[26] Moreover, another consequence of this different focus, as compared to Kolm, is that here all moral theories and rules considered require indeed that mutual cooperation (CC) be ranked first, while not necessarily implying that the *free-rider's* payoff (DC) be ranked second. Whereas, in Kolm's analysis of social states or societies, either CC or DC (Aa or Ae, in his notation) has to be ranked first, and the other second.

In the present context of moral theories, and following Kolm (1983), what, in Section 2, was called *greed* (DC > CC) may be called the (immoral) principle of 'returning evil for good'; and what was called *mistrust* or *fear* (DD > CD) can be said to conform to the idea of 'vengeance' and to the biblical principle of 'an eye for an eye and a tooth for a tooth'. The *absence of greed* (CC > DC) accords with the principle of 'gratitude' toward others and of 'returning good for good' (a principle symmetrical to the previous one of 'vengeance'), and is indeed a necessary (albeit not sufficient) condition for cooperative behaviour. And the *absence of fear* (CD > DD) accords with the Christian precept of 'returning good for evil' or 'turning the other cheek', in place of the old precept of 'an eye for an eye'. Also, CC > DD can now be interpreted as an individual's 'preference for a cooperative society rather than a non-cooperative one' – a preference that all 'cooperative' individuals (as also many 'competitive' ones) strictly have.

Finally, taking together pairs of preferences, one can consider (similarly to Kolm), the following four possibilities:

I. DD > CD & DC > CC: 'preference for personal non-cooperation', given the choice of others whatever that may be.
II. CD > DD & CC > DC: 'preference for personal cooperation', given the choice of others whatever that may be.
III. DD > CD & CC > DC: preference for both 'vengeance' *and* 'gratitude'.
IV. CD > DD & DC > CC: preference for returning 'good for evil' *and* 'evil for good'.

The first set of preferences (based both on the idea of 'vengeance' and of 'returning evil for good') may be called, as Kolm argues, 'pagan' preferences in the biblical sense. In a two-player, two-strategy game, when ranked in particular as DC > CC > DD > CD, they represent the actual preferences of Prisoner's Dilemma players, while when ranked as DC > DD > CC > CD those of Deadlock players. Thus, both the Prisoner's Dilemma and Deadlock can be seen as special cases of a 'pagan' society, one whose members all share the same 'pagan' preferences – or, one may say, of an individualistic, selfish, rational, utility-maximizing, *laissez-faire*, market society, which faithfully but unsuccessfully relies upon the Invisible Hand to bring about cooperation. Indeed, individuals with these 'pagan' preferences do not cooperate (for, as seen in Section 7.2, non-cooperation is their dominant strategy), albeit in the case of the former individual type at least, each would actually prefer a cooperative to a non-cooperative society.

The second set of preferences (the exact opposite to the first, and based both on the idea of 'returning good for evil' and 'returning good for good') may be called 'ethical' preferences. These include, when ranked in particular as CC > DC > CD > DD, what Kolm rightly calls 'Christian' preferences, but which may also be those of a (secular) 'Altruist'. And they include also two other cases: that of 'Kantian' preferences (CC > CD > DD > DC), and that of a 'Cooperator''s preferences (CC > CD > DC > DD). Moreover, this second set embodies a weaker 'ethical' sub-set: DC > DD & CC > CD, which may be called (following Kolm) the 'preference for the cooperation of others', given one's own choice whatever it may be. This subset of preferences – involving the first two conditions for a true dilemma to exist, and implying both a non-cooperator's 'preference for the cooperation of others' (DC > DD), and a cooperator's 'preference for the cooperation of others' (CC > CD) – is present in the preferences of both an 'Altruist' (or 'Christian') and a 'Cooperator', but not in those of a 'Kantian', whose ethics can thus be said to be the strongest. All individuals with 'ethical' preferences do cooperate (with cooperation being indeed their dominant strategy) and thus all enjoy life in an 'ethical' society, whose members all have the same types of ethical preferences.

The third set of preferences (a middle case between the first and second) can be called, as Kolm argues, 'Judaeo-Islamic' or 'biblical' preferences. When they are, moreover, ranked as CC > DC > DD > CD (as in Kolm), their correspondent two-player, two-strategy game would be Stag Hunt. Two other cases are also possible. One is CC > DD > CD > DC, which may be strictly called 'Biblical' preferences, so as to differentiate them from the former, which may be referred to as 'Judaeo-Islamic'; the other is CC > DD > DC > CD which may be called 'Pharisaic' preferences.[27] All individuals with 'biblical' preferences may or may not cooperate, depending on what other people do, or what they each believe the others will do, although they all prefer to live in a cooperative 'biblical' society, rather than in a non-cooperative 'biblical' society.

The fourth and final set of preferences (a case of pure contrariness) may be called, as Kolm suggests, 'mad' preferences, for they 'correspond neither to any widespread behavior pattern nor to any influential moral system'. In the two-player, two-strategy context when ranked as DC > CC > CD > DD, they would actually represent the preferences of Chicken players. Individuals with these 'mad' preferences would indeed live in a 'mad' society, where (as seen in Section 7.2) each individual would always wish to do the opposite of what others do.

The cases considered here are only those in which cooperation is dictated as the standard of conduct. Thus, the types of preference analysed are the three 'ethical' and the three 'biblical' ones, and the corresponding moral rules and individuals can similarly be called 'ethical' or 'biblical'. Each of the six cases is based on a particular set of moral principles, and entails different human motivations or 'subjective preferences'. In each case, moreover, the rules that individuals follow reflect 'internalized' norms of social behaviour, being supported as they are by either religious belief or individual secular ethics. For the underlying moral principles are based on 'transcendental' religious thinking (as in the case of Christian or 'biblical' individuals), or on 'rational' moral grounds (as in the case of Kantians, Cooperators or Altruists).

The general moral principle prescribing cooperation, underlying the three 'ethical' rules, may be called the 'Law of Morality'. More precisely it is, in turn, the principle of (i) Kantian 'duty', (ii) cooperativeness (or 'cooperative utilitarianism') and (iii) ('rational') altruism. The first principle can be seen as an expression of Ethical Liberalism, the second of Rule Utilitarianism, and the third of Ethical Socialism or of Christianity (and of the 'Christian altruistic ethic' in particular). As for the three 'biblical' individuals, the common moral principle may be called the 'Law of Almighty God'. More precisely: (i) the Fear of God and of God's Punishment, reflecting a strictly Biblical-type ethic; and moreover, in the Judaeo-Islamic and Pharisaic cases, (ii) the Love of God and hence the Love of Man, thus also reflecting a 'biblical' altruistic precept, but less pure and seemingly more hypocritical than the Christian one.

The behaviour of 'cooperative' individuals is in accordance with the moral rules they follow and which govern their choices. Specifically, the behaviour of Cooperators (or Rule Utilitarians) and Altruists (or Christians) is informed by the moral criterion of the attainment of the highest possible common well-being, reflecting the instrumental role (rationality) of cooperation. According to Rule Utilitarianism, a Cooperator should follow that rule which, if followed by all, would produce the best outcome from a utilitarian perspective: 'the greatest happiness for the greatest number', as Jeremy Bentham and John Stuart Mill postulated. Thus, a Cooperator will unconditionally cooperate.[28] Following the Socialist or Christian precepts of love and altruism, an Altruist will also cooperate, no matter what other people do, willing to sacrifice his own self-interest to morality for the benefit of society.[29] Kantians' behaviour is informed by the 'categorical imperative' of self-imposed universalizable moral law – which stems from individual autonomy and is dictated by reason alone – reflecting the Kantian deontological value (rationality) of cooperation. Here, the attainment of the highest possible common 'good' is only a fortunate by-product, and not the motivating principle. Lastly, all 'biblical' individuals' behaviour is dictated by the 'Law of God', prescribing love and solidarity – 'You shall love your neighbour as yourself' (Leviticus 19:18)[30] – and promising (or threatening) punishment for greed, unkindness or uncooperativeness. Thus, their behaviour reflects the 'commanded' value-choice of cooperation.

For all 'cooperative' individuals, mutual cooperation is the best outcome, both from a personal and collective perspective; that is, their most preferred choice is to cooperate in a cooperative society (CC). Yet they may not all behave in the same manner. Thus, 'ethical' individuals are *natural* cooperators. The term *natural* well captures the idea that these individuals display an 'unconditional' moral commitment (obligation) to cooperation. They always cooperate, whether or not others do. In game-theoretic terms, cooperation is their *dominant strategy*, as they have no incentive or temptation to defect. Moreover, both from a Kantian and Cooperator's perspective, choosing not to cooperate when others do is worse than choosing to cooperate when others don't (DC < CD). Indeed for a Kantian, who cooperates out of Moral Duty or Moral Law (a principle of 'rational' categorical commitment), choosing to be a lone defector (a traitor or cheater: DC) is the worst possible (if at all conceivable) choice – for, according to Kant, he who is conscious of having *cheated* (at play) must *despise* himself as soon as he compares himself with the moral law. Conversely, both for Cooperators who adhere unconditionally to the cooperative rule, and for Altruists (or Christians) who cooperate out of love and independently of their degree of love for others,[31] the worst possible outcome is mutual defection: to be a non-cooperator in a non-cooperative society (DD). But an Altruist (or Christian) prefers to be a lone defector to a lone cooperator (DC > CD).[32]

In contrast, 'biblical' individuals may be called *command* cooperators. Here, the term *command* reflects the idea that these individuals when cooperating do so (as if) according to God's command or in God's name, and hence out of religious obligation. For unlike *natural* cooperators, to them what others do matters, and so their commitment to cooperation is in a sense 'conditional'. In game-theoretic terms, they have *no dominant strategy*, and have in fact an incentive to defect for fear of betrayal, or, in moral terms, out of 'vengeance' (DD > CD). Although mutual cooperation is also for them clearly better than mutual defection (CC > DD), the latter is their second or third best choice, undoubtedly seen as a sort of 'divine social justice'. In fact, they all prefer to do what other people do: cooperate if others cooperate, and defect if others defect. Yet they may not know what the rest will do, and so face a 'risky' choice. Thus, they may choose to cooperate obeying God's command.[33] In particular, a Biblical individual may cooperate (as if) out of Fear of God and of His Punishment. Indeed, like a Kantian or Cooperator, he prefers to be a lone cooperator than a lone defector (CD > DC). Moreover, like a Kantian but for different reasons, he also sees the latter option (DC) as the worst possible choice: in the case of a Kantian, that choice involves the loss of self-respect and personal dignity, while for a Biblical individual it may involve a sense of 'guilt' for betraying others, and thus the fear of divine punishment. The 'guilty conscience' argument may also clearly apply to the other 'biblical' individuals. These may choose to cooperate (as if) out of Love of God and hence Love of Man. But like Altruists (or Christians), they also prefer to be lone defectors to lone cooperators.[34]

Thus, 'cooperative' individuals' preferences are not the same as in a Prisoner's Dilemma or other Social Dilemmas, but are 'modified' by other (moral) considerations. As one may say, 'extra payoffs' are introduced, altering those facing a 'true' Prisoner's Dilemma player. The six 'cooperative' individuals' characteristics are summarized in Table 7.2 (while a summary comparison between 'competitive' and 'cooperative' individuals, in terms of their payoff orderings and outcomes, is given in Figure 7.1). The common moral principle for all 'cooperative' individuals is that of 'gratitude' (CC > DC). In addition, 'ethical'

if one is simply interested in predicting their conduct, then the answer is 'no' (albeit, one has to remember, 'biblical' individuals cooperate only if God's command is duly obeyed). But if one is also concerned with their subjective preferences, or, more significantly, with what motivates their behaviour (the underlying moral reasons for it), then the answer is surely 'yes'. For, although all 'cooperative' individuals are expected always to choose (spontaneously or on command) to co-operate, they may well react differently to the same circumstances or a change in the environment.

Thus, *religious* ('biblical' and 'Christian') individuals who for some reason were to lose, permanently or perhaps only temporarily, their faith in God (due, for example, to the sudden or cruel loss of a loved one) might, as a result, 'reverse' into Prisoner's Dilemma players. (Although as Joan Robinson (1962) notes: 'If a man's conscience disintegrates when he loses his faith in God, it cannot have set properly when he was young' (pp. 14–15).) Whereas *non-religious* ethical individuals, experiencing the same event, could be expected to carry on with their previous cooperative conduct. Also, 'biblical' individuals might choose to defect, were they ever to form a strong expectation, and so come to the conclusion, that the others are bound not to cooperate. In this case, their fear of being betrayed (and so their sentiment of 'vengeance') would dominate their fear of God, and a 'non-nasty' defection would result, with them resigned to the outcome of (divine) common punishment. While 'ethical' individuals would still cooperate, even when expecting defection by others – either because of their moral duty or obligation to do so, in the case of Kantians, or because of their instrumental commitment to cooperation as the route to the highest possible common welfare, in the case of Cooperators and Altruists (or Christians). And they would still be better off than had they also chosen to defect (since for them CD > DD), according to their maxim of 'returning good for evil'.

'Internalized' norms of cooperative conduct can be the result of religious belief or of individual social ethics independent of religion. Yet the above arguments point (to some extent) to the superiority of individual (secular) morality – the 'Religion of Humanity' in J.S. Mill's words – over (supernatural) religion, in bringing about and sustaining social and economic cooperation – a point also emphasized by several moral philosophers and social thinkers.[36]

The functional or instrumental role of religion in guaranteeing individual cooperation, by way of supporting morality, is undoubtedly very important. Indeed, as Joan Robinson (1962) puts it: 'Morality is desired and respected for its own sake; religion is being recommended to us because it supports morality, not morality because it derives from religion' (p. 15).[37] But the role played by the Law of Morality, not founded on religious belief, may in this respect be even stronger. For here self-interest is not surrendered in the name of God, that is, forgone in obedience to what are perceived to be God's orders or desires: no *deus ex machina* (or 'God-cum-Satan' in Fred Hirsch's (1977) words) is present or required for cooperative behaviour to emerge as the norm. All is needed, but what is also clearly more demanding on the (God-less) individual, is for him to act on some moral principle that prescribes cooperation as the ethically superior conduct – or even as the only acceptable one, in the case of a Kantian.

The moral principle dictating cooperative behaviour can be that of Kantian 'duty', or 'cooperativeness' or 'altruism'.[38] Each of these moral principles puts more or less strong claims on individual 'private' morality, and are certainly stronger than when individual acts are based on religious conviction. For as Hirsch (1977, p. 142) notes: 'Less love of God necessitates more love of Man.' Yet, if any of these moral principles ever motivate human conduct, then social, economic and moral cooperation might well be built on more solid foundations than if it were purely built on religious faith and obligation – for faith might fade away as inexplicably as it presents itself in the first place.

Moreover, the family, the community and society at large may have a more successful role in 'shaping' an individual's moral values, and hence influencing his cooperative behaviour, than in 'converting' the same individual to a religious faith. Thus, although more demanding than religiously-based norms, genuinely ethically-based norms may, in principle, grow more naturally and be nurtured within the social environment.

7.4 SUMMARY

Cooperation can be driven by 'rational' egoistic motivations or material incentives, and indeed standard economic and game-theoretic explanations of cooperative play presuppose self-interested conduct. Yet, choosing to cooperate in a situation such as the unrepeated Prisoner's Dilemma, as many individuals do, is clearly inconsistent with, and cannot be derived from, self-interest, and violates standard conceptions of individual 'rational choice'. Claiming individuals' 'irrationality' is here a possible answer.

However, cooperative behaviour in such a hostile situation can also arise if individuals are actually driven by 'moral' motivations. Thus, the main aim here has been to consider moral principles and rules that prescribe cooperation as the behavioural norm. Six cases have been analysed and their underlying moral principles discussed, with private lay morality and religious belief clearly identified as the two alternative sources of moral cooperative behaviour. And it has finally been suggested that the former type of morality might be superior to the latter in supporting socio-economic cooperation, for it is only based on altruism, duty or cooperativeness and reason, while the latter has to be also based on an ('irrational' and possibly 'volatile') act of faith.

APPENDIX 7.1. DESCRIPTION OF SOCIAL DILEMMAS

In the classic 'Prisoner's Dilemma' story, two men are arrested and charged with a joint serious crime, and held in separate cells. Each can either confess or not confess to that crime. If neither confesses, they are both sentenced only for a minor offence. If both confess, they are both charged with the major crime. If one confesses and the other doesn't, the former goes free while the latter is punished with a heavier sentence. In daily life, the most common type of 'Prisoner's Dilemma' is the 'free-rider' dilemma, where there are many players rather than just two, and the name refers to the dilemma facing public transport users about whether to pay or not for the fare, when there is little chance of being found out, and one may simply hop over the turnstiles.

'Deadlock' seems not to have a classic story, although an example can be some failures to reach bilateral disarmament agreements, when the failure is actually due to a lack of will to disarm on either side.

The original game of 'Chicken' – from the famous 1955 movie with James Dean, *Rebel Without a Cause* – consists of two teenagers driving their stolen cars simultaneously towards the edge of a cliff, jumping out at the last possible moment. The first one to jump out is 'chicken' and hence the loser. (As Rabin (1993) notes, this game 'is widely studied by political scientists, because it captures well situations in which nations challenge each other. Each country hopes to "dare" while the other country backs down . . .; but both dread most of all the outcome (dare, dare) in which neither nation backs down.')

In the two-person version of the classic 'Stag Hunt' story – from Rousseau's (1755) book *A Discourse on Inequality* – two hunters can together hunt a stag or separately catch a hare. But if one runs off chasing hares while the other remains faithfully at his post, the former can catch a few hares, while the latter ends up with nothing.

In the biblical 'Bully' tale, two women both claim to be the mother of a child, and so King Solomon proposes splitting the child in two. While the impostor stands firm, the real mother naturally horrified abandons her claim to the child and is hence awarded the child in virtue of Solomon's renowned wisdom.

APPENDIX 7.2. ASYMMETRIC GAMES AMONG 'COMPETITIVE' PLAYERS

The games here analysed are presented in the bottom part of Table 7.1.

In the game of Bully, one player has the Chicken preferences, while the other the Deadlock's. This game has a Nash equilibrium, in which the Deadlock player (the bully) defects and the Chicken player cooperates (giving in).

Among the other asymmetric games, it is worth noting the first one, where one player has the Prisoner's Dilemma preferences and the other the Deadlock's. Mutual defection is here obviously a Nash dominant equilibrium, as both players' dominant strategy is to defect. But the interesting feature is that the Deadlock player ends up better off in terms of scores than the Prisoner's Dilemma player. The fifth game should also be noticed – a cross between Chicken and Stag Hunt – where, given the two players' preferences (with a greedy Chicken player and a distrustful Stag Hunt player), no 'pure strategy' Nash equilibrium solution exists. A 'pure strategy' is one where each player chooses to either cooperate or defect with certainty. This game has, though, a unique 'mixed strategy' Nash equilibrium, in which each player cooperates with probability 1/2 and defects with probability 1/2. A 'mixed strategy' equilibrium thus implies that players consciously randomize their choices; alternatively, it can be viewed as an 'equilibrium in conjectures' about each other's strategy choices. (It should here be noticed that the game of Chicken actually has a third Nash equilibrium, a 'mixed strategy' one, where, based on Table 7.1 payoffs, both players cooperate (or defect) with probability 1/2.)

In summary, of the six asymmetric 'competitive' games, three games (the first, third and sixth) have a unique Nash 'non-cooperative' equilibrium. This is, moreover, a dominant equilibrium in the first game, and a collectively suboptimal solution in the third game. Two games (the second and fourth (Bully)) have a unique Nash equilibrium where one player defects and the other cooperates; while one game (the fifth) has no 'pure-strategy' Nash equilibrium, though it has a unique 'mixed-strategy' Nash equilibrium.

8 Efficiency and Equity: A Short-Run, Short-Sighted Trade-Off

INTRODUCTION

The relationship between economic efficiency on the one hand and equity, fairness or income distribution on the other represents a critical economic (and social and political) issue. Indeed, it is a key issue not only for individuals' present welfare, as it affects economic activity and performance, but also for economic growth and hence for individuals' future welfare.

Three very recent events highlight the relevance of this matter at both national and international level. First, the publication of the UK's Joseph Rowntree Foundation's report 'Inquiry into Income and Wealth', in February 1995. According to the report, income and wealth inequalities in Britain are now the widest since the war, and the gap between rich and poor has grown during the 1980s faster and further in Britain than in any other comparable industrialized country, except New Zealand. And yet 'There has not been a faster rate of growth in Britain than in previous periods when the gap between rich and poor was smaller.' Also, growing inequality has not encouraged wealth creation, and the British remain worse off than people in richer countries where there is significantly less inequality, and where in recent years inequality has only slightly risen, as, for example, in Germany and France, or where it has in fact fallen, as in Italy. The second event has been the United Nations' conference on poverty, the 'World Summit for Social Development', held in Copenhagen in March 1995. The main aim of the UN conference, to 'completely eradicate poverty', stands in the face of facts: one-fifth of the world's population lives in poverty, with women and children in particular affected – indeed almost half the world's under-fives live in poverty, including increasing numbers within industrialized countries such as the UK.[1] Finally, the United Nations' (1996) 'Human Development Report' dramatically highlights the growing gap between rich and poor countries. According to this report, the total wealth of the world's 358 billionaires is greater than the combined annual incomes of countries with 45 per cent of the world's population – 2.3 billion people. Also, in more recent years, 100 countries have actually suffered economic decline or stagnation which has reduced the income of a quarter of the world's population.[2] Moreover, inequality has grown not only between countries but also within them, as notably in the UK.

In theory, the relationship between economic efficiency and a more equal (or fairer) income distribution can take three forms, reflecting three different hypotheses. Namely, efficiency and equity can be: (i) negatively related, or (ii) independent, or (iii) positively related.

Standard (neoclassical) economic theory normally stresses the first hypothesis, which implies the existence of a choice or trade-off between efficiency and equity, and hence suggests a fundamental dilemma for societies and governments in particular. Mainstream introductory economics textbooks make this point very clear, as a small sample of leading texts shows. Thus, according to Begg, Fischer and Dornbusch (1994), 'there is an inevitable trade-off between the competing objectives of efficiency and equity' (p. 283). 'In practice, governments face a conflict between equity and efficiency' (p. 276). 'Governments that wish to redistribute have to trade-off gains in equity against losses in allocative efficiency because redistributive taxes introduce distortions' (p. 333). According to Parkin and King (1995), 'it is now recognized that there exists what has been called the "big tradeoff" between fairness and economic efficiency' (from Arthur Okun's (1975) book *Equality and Efficiency: The Big Tradeoff*). 'Taking account of the disincentive effects of redistribution and the resource costs of administering the redistribution is what produces the "big tradeoff". A more equally shared pie results in a smaller pie' (pp. 498–9). According to Samuelson and Nordhaus (1992): 'Today, even the most radical socialist recognizes that some differences in economic outcome are necessary if the economy is to function efficiently . . . In taking steps to redistribute income from the rich to the poor, governments may harm economic efficiency and reduce the amount of national income available to distribute' (p. 365), for 'attempts to reduce income inequality by progressive taxation or welfare payments may harm economic incentives to work or save' (p. 373). 'The question of how much we are willing to pay in reduced efficiency for greater equity was addressed by Arthur Okun in his "leaky bucket" experiment . . . suppose the bucket of redistribution has a leak in it . . . Then redistribution in the name of equity has been at the expense of economic efficiency . . . Society must decide how much efficiency to sacrifice to gain greater equality' (pp. 365–6).

The second hypothesis – of independence between efficiency and equity – was, in contrast, supported by classical economists in the last century, who 'believed that inequality was a universal constant, unchangeable by public policy', as Samuelson and Nordhaus note (1992, p. 372). Any attempts to reduce inequality would be ineffective – for income distribution was held to be determined by economic laws, and not by political decisions – and would only probably result in a smaller pie as well as social chaos, in terms of socio-political struggle and class warfare.

However, it is the third hypothesis – of a positive correlation between efficiency and equity (and in turn between economic growth and equity) – that is sustained here. This hypothesis seems to be clearly supported by the Rowntree report, as also by a number of recent academic studies. Specifically, Persson and Tabellini (1994), and Alesina and Rodrik (1994) find a negative theoretical and empirical link between inequality and growth. In particular, Persson and Tabellini, in a work set in the context of both endogenous growth theory and endogenous economic policy theory, conclude that (in democratic countries at least) 'inequality is harmful for growth'. And their empirical work supports their theory, by showing 'a strong negative relation between income inequality at the start of the period and growth in the subsequent period'.[3] In brief, the greater the income inequality, the greater in a democracy is the political demand for redistribution.[4] But, since redistribution has an adverse effect on economic activity (for redistributive taxation across profits has a negative impact on capital accumulation), equilibrium growth is consequently lower. Thus, a more equal income distribution, resulting in less popular demand for redistribution, increases economic growth – as does a higher average level of basic skills, or, more controversially, a reduction in the political rights of the poor or (equivalently) their *de facto* disenfranchisement, since they all imply a richer median voter. And Rodrik (1996), referring to the above works, highlights the importance of a fair income distribution for economic growth, while examining the experience of the East Asian tigers, compared to that of most Latin American, African and Asian countries.[5]

In a work related to the same literature, and which formally captures the *dynamic circular causality* between income distribution and growth, Saint-Paul and Verdier (1993) also study the link between inequality and growth. But in their model, the main instrument of redistribution is public education, which is provided in an egalitarian way and financed by proportional taxation on labour income, and which, moreover, makes income distribution evolve endogenously. Thus, in contrast with the above, they find that, under non-distortionary taxation, and provided that poverty is not correlated with non-participation in the electoral process, 'initial inequality benefits growth because it implies more political support for public education'. Hence, 'redistribution and democratization of a society does not necessarily have adverse effects on growth'. In fact, more public education fosters growth since it is an investment in human capital, and at the same time it increases income equality 'through the equalizing effects of public education on the transmission of intergenerational human capital.' Also, their model implies 'a positive correlation between the growth rate and the speed of income equalization', where the latter is faster, the larger the spending share on education. And it predicts that 'spending on education will eventually decline, and so will the growth rate, as inequality declines'. However, as Persson and Tabellini (1994), they similarly find that, under distortionary taxation, redistribution may not be good for growth. Specifically, in this case an inverted U-shaped relationship between inequality and growth emerges: 'too unequal, or too equal countries will grow less than countries with intermediate levels of inequality'. A very recent work related to the latter, as also to Perotti (1993), is Bénabou (1996). It examines how socio-economic stratification or segregation of individuals into homogeneous communities, as opposed to integration, and how alternative systems of education finance (state, local or private funding) affect inequality and growth. The main result of this analysis, set in a dynamic and stochastic framework, is that 'integration may slow down growth in the short run but nonetheless increase it in the long run, due to its gradual homogenizing effect'. And a move to state funding of education, '[r]edistributing funds to equalize spending across students leads to the same intertemporal trade-off between initial distortions and long-term efficiency gains as integration'.

In this context, the pioneering work of Simon Kuznets (1955, 1966), on the relation between economic development and income distribution, must also clearly be mentioned. According to his hypothesis, also known as the *Kuznets curve*, income inequality will first widen in the early stages of development and then narrow in the later stages. Thus, developed countries should experience a narrowing of income differentials and become more equal societies than less developed countries. The evidence here does indicate that developing countries often have much more unequal income distributions than developed countries. But, as already mentioned, in more recent years and especially since the 1980s, there has been a new growing gap in incomes and between rich

8.4 CAUSALITY BETWEEN EFFICIENCY AND DISTRIBUTION

Another crucial issue concerns the direction of causality between efficiency and distribution, if and when they are positively or negatively related, that is, in Case I or III (not, clearly, in Case II when they are assumed to be independent of each other). In other words, which is the *cause* and which the *effect*? Specifically, the question is: (a) Does efficiency cause distribution? And if so, does it cause a better distribution (Case III), or a worse distribution (Case I)? *Or* (b) Does distribution cause efficiency? And if so, does it cause higher efficiency (Case III), or lower efficiency (Case I)? Yet in other words, does distribution depend on efficiency (hypothesis (a)), or does efficiency depend on distribution (hypothesis (b))?

Here, the Left would normally tend to support hypothesis (b), and clearly Case III, the argument being that better income distribution, and hence better education, health, . . . will benefit the economy by increasing productivity, and so result in efficiency gains and greater economic growth. But the Left may also recognize that greater efficiency will allow for better distribution – as the cake becomes bigger, each individual may gain, and be entitled or aspire to a bigger share – hence partly accepting hypothesis (a). In fact, the Left may well acknowledge a certain degree of interdependence between efficiency and distribution, and may thus even accept Case IIIb or Case IIIc.

By contrast, the Right, when acknowledging a relationship between efficiency and distribution (that is, when not stressing Case II), is more likely to believe in a negative relationship (Case I), and is also more likely to believe that distribution will somehow be determined according to the level of efficiency. That is, the Right would be more likely to support hypothesis (a). But also, if at all supporting a positive relationship (Case III), the Right would quite certainly stress Case IIIb: efficiency gains, at relatively high levels of efficiency, require more inequality, that is, a worse distribution; or else Case IIIc: greater equality, at relatively high levels of equality, implies lower efficiency. Similarly, when more commonly supporting a negative relationship (Case I), the Right would probably stress Case Ib: 'excessive' levels of income equality, that is, a very egalitarian distribution will cause inefficiency (or negative efficiency).

Clearly, another possibility, and perhaps the correct one, is that efficiency and distribution are strictly interdependent, with each one affecting the other: efficiency depends on distribution, that is, on the degree of income equality, and the better the distribution (possibly up to a certain point), the greater the scope for efficiency; but also, at the same time, distribution depends on the level of efficiency, and the greater the efficiency, the greater the scope for better distribution.

∴ Efficiency and equity are each *cause and effect* of the other.

8.5 ECONOMY'S TRAJECTORY

Related to the issue of the direction of causality is the issue of the economy's trajectory, or time path. Here, two questions can be asked. First, given the economy's starting point (the initial conditions), where will the economy end up? Also and second, how will the economy reach an optimal or desired position?

In order to analyse this issue, it is possible to construct the economy's *phase diagram* in (e, d) space, as given in Figure 8.2. Efficiency is measured along the vertical axis, while distribution is along the horizontal axis. The intersection of the two axes divides the economy in four Regions. In the top part of the diagram (Regions I and II) efficiency is high ($\hbar$e), while it is low (ℓe) in the bottom part (Regions III and IV). By contrast, distribution is equitable or high ($\hbar$d) on the right-hand side of the diagram (Regions I and IV), while it is inequitable or low (ℓd) on the left-hand side (Regions II and III). Therefore, Region I represents an area of high efficiency and high distribution, and Region III on the contrary an area of low efficiency and low distribution. Whereas Regions II and IV are areas of $\hbar$e-ℓd and ℓe-$\hbar$d, respectively.

Each Region can be said to represent a particular scenario. Specifically:

- Region I. *Socialists'(Poor) ideal (utopia)*: all Rich. An efficient and very equitable (altruistic and cooperative (stable?)) outcome.
- Region II. *Capitalists'(Rich) ideal (reality)*: few Rich and many Poor. An efficient but highly inequitable (selfish and non-cooperative (unstable?)) outcome.
- Region III. *South American (and increasingly Anglo-Saxon) way*: few Rich and majority Poor. An inefficient and very inequitable outcome.
- Region IV. *Socialism in reverse (Africa)*: all Poor. An inefficient but very equitable outcome.

In relation to the first question raised above, it is possible to consider what would happen to the economy if it were ever to start in each of the four Regions, assuming no government intervention or any policy change. Various potential paths can be envisaged. Thus, if the economy starts, respectively, in:

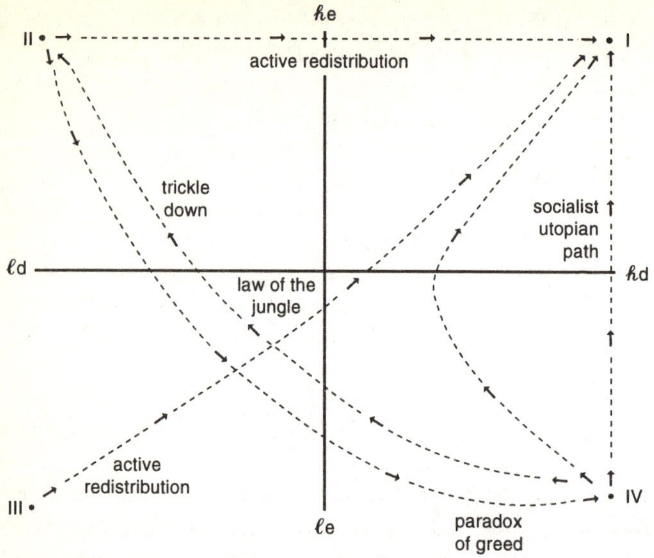

Figure 8.2 The Economy's Four Regions

Note The paths shown by the arrows illustrate some of the conceivable (possible or likely) trajectories of the economy, with or without government intervention, when starting from Regions II, III or IV, and assuming that Region I is the optimal or desired region.

Region I: would it be stable?
Region II: would it move to Region III? And then to Region IV (*paradox of greed*)?
Region III: would it move to Region IV? *Or else* to Region II?
Region IV: would it move to Region I? No! *Hence* to Region III (*law of the jungle*)? And then to Region II (*trickle-down*)? *Or* would it be stable?

In relation to the second question raised above, if, as may well be the case, Region I is the optimal or desired region, the economy might reach it:

1. If, by chance (or luck), it starts in Region I (globally stable?).
2. If it starts in Region IV:
   (a) with no government intervention:
      1. if the *law of the jungle* ensues moving the economy to Region III,

   2. if the *trickle-down* factor follows, with free-market greedy incentives, moving the economy from Region III to II,
   3. finally, with intervention – *redistribution policy* (↑d) – to move the economy from Region II to I;
  (b) with government intervention:
   1. if incentives are provided and equality diminished, moving the economy to Region II (possibly passing through Region III),
   2. with active redistribution policy to move the economy from Region II to I;
  (c) with heavy government intervention:
   ⇒ moving the economy straight to Region I (*socialist utopian trajectory?*), or
   ⇒ moving the economy directly to Region I but with a bent curve, by decreasing income equality.
3. If it starts in Region II:
   with an active redistribution policy, moving the economy directly to Region I; otherwise the economy will move to Region III and then to Region IV, in virtue of the *paradox of greed.*

(Quite certainly, Region II is highly (or globally) unstable, for it causes a sense of injustice and unfairness, thus social unrest, growing criminality and theft, and provokes inefficiency, so that the economy moves to Region III. In other words, Region II cannot be maintained in the long run, but is only a short-run area. As noted, Region II is the selfish Rich ideal and/or the Right (neoclassical) ideology/dogma: high efficiency requires unequal distribution to provide incentives – as underlined by the belief in either the negative relationship between efficiency and equity (downward-sloping Case I), or in the positive but bent-curve relationship (upward-sloping Case IIIb).)

4. If it starts in Region III:
   with an active redistribution policy (↑d) ⇒ greater efficiency (↑e), moving the economy to Region I (probably passing through Region IV).

Finally, it may here be noticed that Region I (the area of high efficiency and equitable income distribution) is, conceivably, the optimal and desired region for (at least) all the following:

- benevolent government/ruler who regards all individuals as equal,
- socialist ruler/dictator,
- egalitarians/socialists,
- Catholic believers,
- altruistic and/or cooperative Rich.

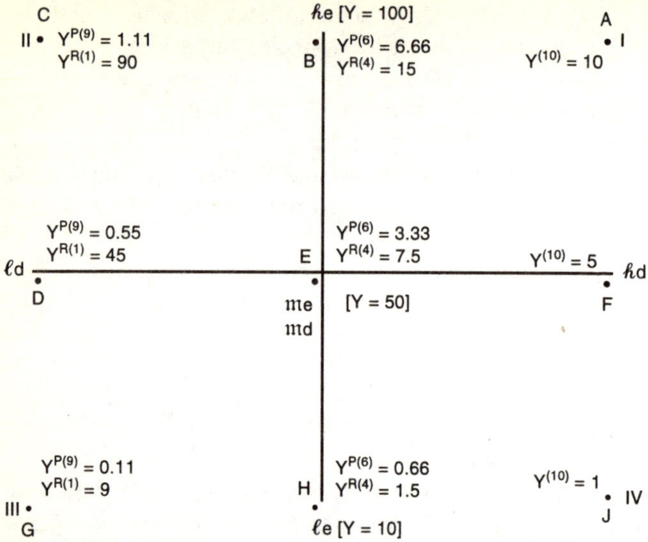

Figure 8.3 Ten Individuals' Income Distribution

Note The numbers in superscript parentheses for each individual income level indicate the number of individuals receiving that particular income.

8.6 INCOME DISTRIBUTION IN THE FOUR REGIONS: A SIMPLE MODEL

Income distribution in each of the four Regions (as well as along the axes) is here analysed using a simple theoretical model, and is illustrated in Figure 8.3. Society is assumed to consist of just ten individuals. Both efficiency and distribution can vary between high and low levels.

When the economy operates at high efficiency levels, output/income (Y) is high. On the other hand, low efficiency level results in low output/income, and medium efficiency (on the ℓd–ℏd line) in a medium output/income. Specifically, here in the limit: ℏe ⇒ ℏY [Y=100]; 𝔪e ⇒ 𝔪Y [Y=50]; ℓe ⇒ ℓY [Y=10].

High distribution here means an equitably distributed income. Low distribution is, conversely, assumed to mean that 90 per cent of the poorer population gets only ten per cent of income, with the remaining ten per cent of richer people getting 90 per cent of income.[13] And a medium distribution (on the ℏe–ℓe line) is taken to mean that 60 per cent of individuals get 40 per cent of income, whilst the other 40 per cent of richer people get 60 per cent of income. Specifically, in the limit: ħd ⇒ each individual has equal Y [$Y_i = 0.1Y$, $\Sigma_i Y_i = Y$; $i = 1, \ldots, 10$]; ɱd ⇒ 6 Poor get 40 per cent Y [$Y^P_i = 0.067Y$, $\Sigma_i Y^P_i \equiv Y^P = 0.4Y$; $i = 1, \ldots, 6$] *and* 4 Rich get 60 per cent Y [$Y^R_j = 0.15Y$, $\Sigma_j Y^R_j \equiv Y^R = 0.6Y$; $j = 7, \ldots, 10$]; and ℓd ⇒ 9 Poor get 10 per cent Y [$Y^P_i = 0.011Y$, $\Sigma_i Y^P_i \equiv Y^P = 0.1Y$; $i = 1, \ldots, 9$] *and* 1 (only) Rich gets 90 per cent Y [$Y^R_{j=10} \equiv Y^R = 0.9Y$]. Therefore, at any efficiency level, ɱd ⇒ $Y^R_j = 2.25Y^P_i$ and $Y^R = 1.5Y^P$; whereas ℓd ⇒ $Y^R_{j=10} = 81Y^P_i$ and $Y^R = 9Y^P$.

Moreover, notice, the share of total income going to the individual Rich (Poor) is nine times as high under ℓd (ħd) as under ħd (ℓd), six times as high under ℓd (ɱd) as under ɱd (ℓd), and 1.5 times as high under ɱd (ħd) as under ħd (ɱd). Therefore, it is obvious that, for any efficiency and hence income level, the Rich and Poor preferences over income distribution are totally opposed. However, whether the Rich (Poor) are actually better off under ℓd (ħd) than ħd (ℓd) or ɱd, or else under ɱd than ħd (ℓd), depends on the specific level of efficiency and hence output/income.[14]

Figure 8.3 illustrates the income distribution for the ten individuals in the limiting points of each of the four Regions, as well as on the extreme points along the two axes and at the intersection of the axes (nine points altogether). Specifically, for each efficiency level, income distribution at each point is as follows:[15]

ħe	(ħd) Pt A (in Reg.I)	⇒ $Y_i = 10$, $i = 1, \ldots, 10$ ($Y = 100$).
	(ɱd) Pt B (on ħe–ℓe)	⇒ $Y^P_i = 6.66$, $i = 1, \ldots, 6$ ($Y^P = 40$); *and* $Y^R_j = 15$, $j = 7, \ldots, 10$ ($Y^R = 60$).
	(ℓd) Pt C (in Reg.II)	⇒ $Y^P_i = 1.11$, $i = 1, \ldots, 9$ ($Y^P = 10$); *and* $Y^R_{10} = 90$.
ɱe	(ℓd) Pt D (on ℓd–ħd)	⇒ $Y^P_i = 0.55$, $i = 1, \ldots, 9$ ($Y^P = 5$); *and* $Y^R_{10} = 45$.
	(ɱd) Pt E (at inters.)	⇒ $Y^P_i = 3.33$, $i = 1, \ldots, 6$ ($Y^P = 20$); *and* $Y^R_j = 7.5$, $j = 7, \ldots, 10$ ($Y^R = 30$).
	(ħd) Pt F (on ℓd–ħd)	⇒ $Y_i = 5$, $i = 1, \ldots, 10$ ($Y = 50$).
ℓe	(ℓd) Pt G (in Reg.III)	⇒ $Y^P_i = 0.11$, $i = 1, \ldots, 9$ ($Y^P = 1$); *and* $Y^R_{10} = 9$.
	(ɱd) Pt H (on ħe–ℓe)	⇒ $Y^P_i = 0.66$, $i = 1, \ldots, 6$ ($Y^P = 4$); *and* $Y^R_j = 1.5$, $j = 7, \ldots, 10$ ($Y^R = 6$).
	(ħd) Pt J (in Reg.IV)	⇒ $Y_i = 1$, $i = 1, \ldots, 10$ ($Y = 10$).

Focusing, first, on the Rich and Poor situation in the four Regions' limiting cases (Points A,C,G,J), two points seem worth noticing. Firstly:

- the Rich are worse off at G in Region III [Y = 9] than at A in Region I [Y = 10];
- the Poor are worse off at J in Region IV [Y = 1] than at C in Region II [Y = 1.11].[16]

Secondly and more generally, Rich and Poor respective *income ranking* is as follows:

- Rich: C [Reg. II: Y = 90]; A [Reg. I: Y = 10]; G [Reg. III: Y = 9]; J [Reg. IV: Y = 1].
- Poor: A [Reg. I: Y = 10]; C [Reg. II: Y = 1.11]; J [Reg. IV: Y = 1]; G [Reg. III: Y = 0.11].

Also, society's (extreme) choices in terms of both efficiency level and income distribution can be modelled as a *Prisoner's Dilemma*-type game between Rich and Poor. In theory, there are two possible scenarios (a) and (b) depending upon who decides what. These are illustrated, in turn, by Tables 8.1 and 8.2. Each game's 'payoff-matrix' shows the two players' two strategies and related payoffs, with the first (second) entry in each cell giving the payoff for the individual Poor (Rich).

Scenario (a) represents a society in which the Poor work and determine efficiency (Poor choose e), while the Rich govern and determine distribution (Rich choose d). The natural outcome here is that the Poor work hard, while the Rich are greedy, implying capitalist exploitation. Thus, Region II emerges as the equilibrium (upper right cell, boldface), with the Poor receiving an individual income of 1.11 (and a group income of 10) and the (only) Rich an income of 90. Formally, the Poor *dominant* strategy is cooperation ($\hbar$e), whilst the Rich *dominant* strategy is non-cooperation (ℓd), and the outcome is ($\hbar$e, ℓd), that is, Point C in Region II.[17] But this is, as noted, a highly unstable outcome.

Scenario (b), on the contrary, represents a society where the Rich determine the efficiency level (Rich choose e) while the Poor determine distribution (Poor choose d). Here, both Rich and Poor *dominant* strategy is cooperation ($\hbar$e and $\hbar$d, respectively).[18] Hence, equilibrium outcome (upper left cell, boldface) is ($\hbar$e, $\hbar$d), that is, Point A in Region I, where everyone receives an equal income of 10. This is, moreover, a stable outcome. But, unfortunately, this is not a realistic scenario, since the Rich may well determine efficiency, but the Poor are unlikely to determine income distribution.

Thus, scenario (a) is the realistic one. Accordingly, a free-market, competitive, capitalist economy settles in Region II, even if this is

Table 8.1. Rich–Poor 'Game' over (e, d): Scenario (a)

		Rich	
		ħd	ℓd
Poor	ħe	I 10 10	II **1.11 90**
	ℓe	1 1 IV	0.11 9 III

Table 8.2. Rich–Poor 'Game' over (e, d): Scenario (b)

		Rich	
		ħe	ℓe
Poor	ħd	I **10 10**	IV 1 1
	ℓd	1.11 90 II	0.11 9 III

only a short-run (unstable) equilibrium and not a long-run equilibrium. The economy is, in fact, likely (sooner or later) to move to Region III as efficiency declines; and then it may well move to Region IV where everyone is similarly poor, as illustrated by the *paradox of greed*.

Considering, more generally, the Rich and Poor condition at all nine points, their individual *income ranking* in descending order is, respectively, as follows:

• Rich	Pt:	C	D	B	A	G	E	F	H	J
	Y:	90	45	15	10	9	7.5	5	1.5	1
• Poor	Pt:	A	B	F	E	C	J	H	D	G
	Y:	10	6.66	5	3.33	1.11	1	0.66	0.55	0.11

Moreover, Rich and Poor choices in terms of both efficiency and distribution can similarly be analysed in a *Prisoner's Dilemma*-type context. Here, only scenario (a) is considered, where the Poor choose the level of efficiency (ħe, ɱe, ℓe) and the Rich choose the distribution of income (ħd, ɱd, ℓd). Table 8.3 depicts this game: the 'payoff-matrix' now shows the two players' three strategies and related payoffs. The equilibrium outcome of the game (upper right cell, boldface) is the same as before (Table 8.1), with the Poor *dominant* strategy being cooperation (ħe), and the Rich *dominant* strategy non-cooperation (ℓd). Therefore, the solution is (ħe, ℓd), that is, Point C in Region II.

Table 8.3. Rich–Poor 'Three-strategy Game' over (e, d): Scenario (a)

		Rich					
		ħd		md		ℓd	
	ħe	I 10	10	6.66	15	**1.11**	**90** II
Poor	me	5	5	3.33	7.5	0.55	45
	ℓe	1 IV	1	0.66	1.5	0.11	9 III

A final point should be made here. Clearly, for a given efficiency level and hence for a given output/income level, Rich and Poor are in conflict. The Rich favour less equality (ℓd), while the Poor naturally favour more equality (ħd). In fact, theirs is, in this situation, a *zero-sum game*: more to the Rich means less to the Poor, and *vice versa*. However, if – as here argued – income increases not only with efficiency, but also with equity, then a fairer income distribution implies a higher level of income, and also (as is likely) a higher rate of economic growth. Thus, in this circumstance, Rich and Poor need not be in conflict any more, as theirs is now a *non-zero-sum game*. Here, indeed 'a more equally shared pie results in a bigger pie', contrary to the standard neoclassical view generally underlined in leading economics textbooks (as in the already-quoted Parkin and King (1995)).

Obviously though, a conflict of interests between Rich and Poor may persist, even in the latter situation, if the Rich are more interested in their *relative* income position, rather than in their *absolute* income position. That is, if it is the income differential, or gap, between them (Rich) and the Poor that matters to them above all.

8.7 CONCLUSIONS

The conflict between equality and efficiency represents, according to Okun (1975), 'our biggest socioeconomic tradeoff . . . We can't have our cake of market efficiency and share it equally.' Such a view has long been held by economists, and is still maintained by mainstream neoclassicists. Societies and governments have thus to choose how much efficiency to trade-off against greater equality. Moreover, in the society's pursuit of higher economic output and income, this view of a choice or trade-off between efficiency and equity seems to clearly favour the Rich, and is hence generally (and naturally) sustained by the Right.

Redistribution is supposed to harm economic activity, through its distortionary effects on labour supply and capital accumulation. Income differentials are needed in order to provide incentives to work and save, and hence to enhance economic performance and growth.[19] Also and at the same time, income inequalities are regarded as a possibly unfortunate but unavoidable and essential ingredient of *laissez-faire*, free-market, capitalist economies.

This hypothesis – of a negative link between efficiency and equity – has been discussed here alongside its two alternative hypotheses – respectively, of independence, and of a positive correlation between equality and efficiency (and in turn between equality and economic growth). Indeed, the main aim of this chapter has been to highlight the key arguments or reasons underpinning each hypothesis, and not only from an economic perspective, but also, and possibly even more importantly in this context, from a political perspective. Thus, the issue of the shape of the relationship between economic efficiency and income distribution has been debated, as well as the issue of the direction of causation between them (including the possibility of circular causality), and the issue of the economy's trajectories or paths when starting from a particular position, in terms of initial efficiency and equity, or when attempting to attain a particular (optimal or desired) position. Finally, a simple model was developed to analyse the theoretical income distribution within a small society, according to both the level of efficiency and the degree of income inequality. The likely outcome of a 'Prisoner's Dilemma'-type situation between Rich and Poor (when choosing, respectively, income distribution and efficiency) was then considered. As the analysis suggests, in the absence of any government intervention the outcome to be expected is the typical capitalist (exploitation) outcome, of a very efficient but highly inequitable society, with a few rich and the majority poor. But this is probably only a short-run (unstable) equilibrium, since widespread poverty and hence growing social unrest and rising inefficiency are likely to move the economy from this region, eventually toward an economic position of 'Socialism in reverse', where everyone is equal but poor – a result captured by the *paradox of greed*. In other words, high (and growing) income inequality is likely to lead to social and economic instability, mainly due to its potential adverse effects on health, education and crime, hence damaging the long-run prospects of the economy and leading to both a lower level of income and a lower rate of economic growth.

Whether or not redistributive policies introduce distortions, especially on labour supply and the incentives for physical and human capital accumulation, hence reducing economic efficiency and growth, may well be more of an empirical matter than a theoretical one. Here the evidence so far does not seem to yield clear-cut implications. However, the hypothesis that greater equality benefits economic activity and growth seems to have at least as much theoretical foundation as the opposite hypothesis of a trade-off between them. And several sources (already mentioned) provide positive support for it. In particular, some recent academic studies have found that inequality is harmful for growth, both on theoretical and empirical grounds. And, as the 1995 Rowntree Report on income and wealth inequalities notes in relation to the UK experience during the 1980s: 'There is no evidence that the widening income gap increased economic growth.' Moreover, as the World Bank's (1995) 'World Development Report' highlights, what the developing world needs, apart from strong trade unions and better working standards and practices, is greater equality. In fact, according to the report, big inequalities, far from being the inevitable by-product of market economics, represent a barrier to rising prosperity and growth. And according to the OECD's (1996) 'Employment Outlook', growing income inequality may also threaten the societies and stability of industrialized countries.

Finally, in a recent study on efficiency, equity and poverty alleviations, Bardhan (1996) considers the policy debate issue 'on the relative importance of market-driven growth as it trickles down to the poor as opposed to a programme of massive and direct intervention to help the poor'. Thus, many poverty alleviation programmes have involved market distortions, with counter-productive effects both in terms of efficiency and equity and a deleterious impact on growth. On the other hand, as the Southeast Asian experience indicates, 'market-driven economic growth need not be inconsistent with poverty alleviation'. Also, 'there are many projects which by relieving the severe constraints faced by the poor and improving their conditions can help economic growth in the process. This runs somewhat contrary to the preoccupation of mainstream economics with the equity–efficiency trade-off, with its emphasis on the various costs of redistribution in terms of reduced economic incentives and performance . . . There are, however, many situations, particularly in poor countries, when this famous trade-off may be false or at least exaggerated' (pp. 1344–6).[20]

Concluding Notes

The book has not proposed a new economic theory, nor is it going to propose it now. That was not the scope of the book, whose intended aim was merely to discuss a number of ethical issues of relevance to the discipline.

As a closing line, the main characteristics of individuals, firms and markets according to mainstream *neoclassical* economics are here briefly summarized and compared to the corresponding *ethical* ones, so as to emphasize their crucial differences. Some (possibly most) people may clearly regard both versions as extreme cases, and the more realistic lying somewhere in between. Yet one may also reply that it all depends on one's view of 'human nature' and society, and that while at present, at least, the *ethical* types are mainly just an idealized and utopian breed, believing in their possible existence and survival is already a first step toward their actual realization, and certainly an extremely worthy cause to fight for. For without ideals, what would be the meaning and purpose of human life?

ECONOMIC MAN VERSUS ETHICAL MAN

Homo economicus is the individual agent at the centre of neoclassical economic theory (a utilitarian, hedonistic and self-centred, rationalist and individualist ethical theory). He is a selfish, rational, utility maximizer. He acts independently and non-cooperatively, as an isolated social atom with no sense of community or society, and his behaviour is strictly motivated by narrow self-interest. Economic man is a materialistic, totally unemotional and coolly calculating human being: he is a 'rational egoist'. His preferences are set and stable, and he only derives utility or satisfaction from consumption of goods and services and from leisure. Hence work is to him a 'disutility', a pain which has to be endured to earn the pleasures of income and leisure. He is in theory amoral and asocial – albeit he often appears, in practice, to be rather immoral/unethical and markedly anti-social – and his view of others is a mirror image of his own.

In a more extreme version, which seems to dominate modern economics, the troublesome activities of *homo economicus* include, in Oliver

Williamson's (1985, p. 51) words, 'the full set of *ex ante* and *ex post* efforts to lie, cheat, steal, mislead, disguise, obfuscate, feign, distort and confuse'. Thus, as Bowles and Gintis (1993, p. 84) put it: 'The new economic man is not a Victorian gentleman: he is uncompromisingly thorough in pursuing objectives, and often is less benign' than the old one. Indeed, he appears to be living in Hobbes's (1651) 'state of nature' or jungle, that is, in a permanent state of warfare, where *homo homini lupus* and life is 'solitary, poor, nasty, brutish, and short' (p. 107).

Modern *homo economicus* is ruthlessly rational, greedy and opportunistic; he cannot be trusted and mistrusts others, is incapable of commitment and will always free-ride; he regards his selfishness and all his other characteristics and his own behaviour as natural. Only threats of sanctions or punishment and financial inducements may influence him – hence the law has to be invoked to give threats credibility, and appropriate market incentives have to be devised and legal restrictions imposed, in order for him to behave in a socially acceptable, if not desirable, manner. He must hire lawyers to draw up contracts and accountants to check that he has been paid. Legal coercion is also needed to restrain his naturally aggressive behaviour, and indeed his tendency to use force or power to manipulate and/or exploit others to his own advantage.

The nature of *homo ethicus* is completely different and indeed opposite to that of *homo economicus*. He is an altruistic and cooperative individual, honest and truth-telling, trusty and who trusts others. He derives moral and emotional well-being from honouring his obligations to others, has a strong sense of duty and a strong commitment to social goals. He is a natural 'team-player', able to coordinate effectively his actions with those of others and to work in mutually beneficial partnership with others. He regards reciprocity as natural, albeit not a necessary reason for him not to free-ride or behave in the collective interest. Also, as Casson (1990) notes: 'Ethical man is social, and indeed gregarious, whereas economic man is not' (p. 23).

He is intelligent, purposeful and rational, but his purposes and rationality are not the same as those of economic man, and he may in fact be called a 'rational altruist'. Thus, his goals are wider than the simple pursuit of selfish and materialistic objectives, as he values human qualities such as friendship, love, dignity, autonomy, self-respect and respect for others, social justice, fairness and equity. His subjective preferences may change, and he regards work not just as a pain to be endured in exchange for the pleasure of income and leisure, but also as a major source itself of personal satisfaction. Ethical man carefully assesses his own objectives, and not only the means to achieve them, and never treats others simply as means to his own ends. Hence his optimizing behaviour is more complex than simple calculation, and his rationality goes well beyond self-interested utility-maximization. He naturally exchanges gifts with others; he can trade with them by a 'handshake', and can transact informally. Moral reasoning and persuasion are normally sufficient to make him behave in a socially desirable way, without need of threats or pecuniary rewards.

Homo ethicus thinks of other people as similar to himself. He is attentive to their needs and desires, and takes into account both the effect of his own decisions on others, as well as their responses to his own actions. He takes a much wider perspective of problems and situations, than does economic man, and is fully aware of the endogeneity of his own and other people's preferences, norms and behaviour to the system. Indeed, ethical man enjoys a long and meaningful life in a benign, friendly, just and equitable society.

NEOCLASSICAL FIRMS VERSUS ETHICAL FIRMS

The *neoclassical firm* is only profit-motivated, and indeed regards profit maximization as its one and only social responsibility. For its only obligation or moral duty is to the firm's owners or shareholders, and it is to use all its resources efficiently. The firm's pursuit of maximum profit will also, in its view, maximize society's overall economic welfare, due to the working of the Invisible Hand. The firm is fiercely competitive with respect to other firms, and will use very aggressive and even possibly immoral means, to gain or improve its market share, or even to eliminate its competitors so as to get a dominant position. But, in some situations, the firm will also try to collude with other firms at the expense of consumers, although it will normally be difficult to enforce the collusive agreements, as each firm can be expected to free-ride on the others. The modern neoclassical firm has to employ supervisors to carefully monitor its workers, as they cannot be trusted, are not loyal or committed to the firm, and will naturally slack when not supervised. It has, moreover, to give its workers sufficient monetary rewards to induce them to supply the required level of effort, through performance-based contracts and ever more sophisticated performance-related pay schemes; as well as constantly threatening them with financial (and non-financial) sanctions, including the ultimate one of dismissal.

The profit motive is relevant for the *ethical firm* too, since a certain standard of profitability has to be satisfied as a necessary condition for the firm's economic survival and success, and for it to be able to discharge its obligation to its shareholders. But the firm has also other social responsibilities to its employees, consumers, suppliers, creditors and even competitors, besides its shareholders. That is, its obligation is to all its 'stakeholders', and moreover to the local community and society in general, as well as to the environment, in virtue of its economic, social and political power. The modern ethical firm is competitive but also cooperative: it does not collude with other firms at the expense of consumers, but cooperates beneficially with them in the pooling of resources and expertise, as in R&D. The firm does not need to employ supervisors and can thus avoid costly, difficult and imperfect monitoring, as it can trust its workers, who are committed and loyal. Their work motivation and effort is, in fact, high as they all share the firm's general objectives, and moreover receive mutually-agreed fair and equitable remuneration.

NEOCLASSICAL MARKETS VERSUS ETHICAL MARKETS

Neoclassical markets are natural institutions, ethically-neutral – amoral and apolitical, 'colour-blind' and 'accent-deaf' – and indeed neutral arbiters (neither just nor unjust) in the active resolution of conflicts of interest. Neoclassical, competitive and unregulated free-markets are merely allocative mechanisms which operate perfectly well in a self-regulating manner, and indeed provide efficient/optimal solutions to all economic problems. Market exchanges/transactions take place within the anonymity of the market, and property rights underpin the market system also guaranteeing its efficient/optimal working. Neoclassical markets are beneficent and benign institutions. They call for a 'minimal state', as they can rely upon the help of the 'invisible hand', to achieve the most efficient, Pareto-optimal and hence socially desirable economic outcome. Indeed, any government intervention in their operation is an interference, which is likely to cause more harm than good, and should hence be avoided or limited as much as possible, as *laissez-faire* is best.

Ethical markets are, by contrast, historico-socio-political and cultural as well as economic institutions. They reflect and are influenced by the morality of individuals and society as a whole, and their morality in turn affects individuals' choices and behaviour. They are disciplinary institutions, also performing competing claim enforcement as well as allocative functions. They operate quite imperfectly, leading to inefficient outcomes and potentially pervasive market failures. They call for government intervention in the economy and regulation of business activities to correct for market distortions, improve economic performance and protect individuals or groups from exploitation or abuse. Thus they require the 'visible hand of government' alongside the 'invisible hand' of markets, due to the limits of the 'invisible hand' in promoting the general good. But they also require and foster social norms beneficial to the efficient/optimal solution of conflicts of interest, coordination problems and a generally harmonious working of the economy and society in general.

***

Moral values and norms such as altruism, cooperation, solidarity, trust, honesty, truth-telling, obligation, duty, commitment, restraint, non-aggression, social justice, fairness, equity: these are the main values of ethical man, of an ethical firm and ethical markets. And only through their existence, survival and evolution can the 'bad and barbarian' society ultimately be displaced, and a 'good and civilized society' prosper in its place.

Notes

INTRODUCTION

1. Among notable and well-known 'anomalies' or 'irrationalities', one can include: actions likely to produce self-sacrifice, charitable giving, voluntary work, blood donation, voting, paying taxes, 'excessive' saving, working hard, buying lottery tickets, leaving tips. Also, as Frank (1996) notes: 'What the narrow rational choice model cannot explain is the willingness to speak out at personal cost even when doing so will make no difference' (p. 117), and will often involve reputational costs. Thus, as Frank argues: 'Failure to explain such behaviour[s] must be reckoned as a serious shortcoming of narrow rational choice models' (p. 117).
2. Also, as Sen (1987) asks: 'Why should it be *uniquely* rational to pursue one's own self-interest to the exclusion of everything else? It may not, of course, be at all absurd to claim that maximization of self-interest is not irrational, at least not necessarily so, but to argue that anything other than maximizing self-interest must be irrational seems altogether extraordinary.' Indeed 'The self-interest view of rationality involves *inter alia* a firm rejection of the 'ethics-related' view of motivation' (p. 15).
3. As Sen (1987) remarks, 'to deny that people always behave in an exclusively self-interested way is not the same as asserting that they *always* act selflessly. It would be extraordinary if self-interest were not to play quite a major part in a great many decisions, and indeed normal economic transactions would break down if self-interest played no substantial part at all in our choices . . . The real issue is whether there is plurality of motivations, or whether self-interest *alone* drives human beings' (p. 19).
4. As Hargreaves Heap (1993) notes: 'The popular methodology of economics is an ersatz form of empiricism which most economists think (falsely) derives some authority because it is taken from the natural sciences. Instrumental rationality fits with this methodological position very well' (p. 87). However, 'theory in the social world, by affecting what we think, helps to make the world it studies and there is no equivalent to this in the natural sciences. And once we allow for this difference, it will be difficult to sustain some of the popular methodological principles in economics. In particular, the simple positive/normative distinction and the near exclusive reliance on a form of statistical empirical testing both rely on the kind of independence between theory and the object of that theory, which . . . only . . . make(s) sense in the natural world' (p. 88). Also, as Hodgson (1993) argues: 'Clearly, the assumption of maximizing behaviour, or individual rationality, has come to dominate economic theory even to the extent that for many it defines the subject . . . economics is typically defined in terms of its methodology and basic assumptions. This is unusual for a science, to define itself not in terms of its appropriate object of analysis – in this case the economy – but by its chosen box of theoretical tools. Amongst these, rationality has pride of place, along with the associated techniques of